This book is registered with,

United Kingdom Intellectual Property Office
(Registration reference: 66fada23-DMCW-21f-8ed483).

United States Copyright Office
(Registration reference: 1-14311418801)

Published by
Randolph Fenton

Printed in
United Kingdom

DISCLAIMER

The content of *No Shortcuts* is intended for informational and inspirational purposes only. The advice, reflections, and stories shared are based on personal experience and should not replace professional guidance in areas like medical, psychological, legal, or financial matters. Readers are encouraged to consult qualified professionals before making decisions that may impact their health, well-being, or financial stability.

The results and outcomes discussed are illustrative and not guaranteed. Individual experiences and circumstances vary, and the author makes no promise that readers will achieve the same results by applying the ideas or strategies described.

This book references films, musical compositions, and other media under fair use for educational and illustrative purposes. The author does not own the rights to these works, nor does their inclusion imply any affiliation or endorsement by their creators or producers.

The cultural, philosophical, and historical insights, including Stoic and Taoist teachings, are interpretations meant to inspire reflection and growth. These perspectives may not fully align with every reader's understanding or all interpretations of these traditions. By reading this book, you acknowledge that the author is not liable for any actions taken based on its content. It is your responsibility to evaluate and apply the insights in a manner that suits your personal circumstances and professional advice.

ENHANCE YOUR READING EXPERIENCE

For a fully immersive journey through *No Short Cuts*, scan the QR code or visit www.noshortcuts.co.uk/noshortcuts-media.

The playlist is arranged in *exactly the same order* as the music and film references in the book, allowing you to experience each piece naturally as you read. Using your phone alongside the paperback means you won't need to flip back and forth - keeping your focus on the story and enjoying a smooth, uninterrupted flow.

How to Use:

1. Scan the QR code or go to www.noshortcuts.co.uk/noshortcuts-media.

2. Click on the artist or scene image to play the soundtrack or clip in sync with your reading.

With this synchronized playlist, *No Short Cuts* comes to life, blending sound and visuals perfectly with each section of the book.

ACKNOWLEDGEMENTS

Writing *No Shortcuts* has been a transformative task, and I am sincerely grateful to those of influence and to those whose stories of courage and transformation were considerately woven into vital parts of this book.

To the great artists who left indelible impressions on my life: *Pat Metheny, Gustav Holst, Gershwin, Sibelius, Satie, Beethoven, Miles Davis, Hendrix, Antonio Carlos Jobim, Earl Klugh, Luther Vandross, Bee Gees, David Sanborn, Dusty Springfield, Toots Thielemans, Quincy Jones, Eurythmics, ABBA, a-ha, Joe Sample, Level 42, The Police, The Jacksons, Tears for Fears, The Carpenters, Burt Bacharach, Shirley Bassey, Ramsey Lewis, Elton John, Bob James, George Benson, George Michael, David Bowie, The Beatles, T. Rex,* and so many others.

To my mother – Your love, guidance, and resilience have shaped my life. I am forever grateful.
To my sons – I am immensely proud of you all.
Your creativity, kindness, intelligence and maturity are everything I could hope for.
To Yufei – my sincere thanks for your incomparable authenticity and unwavering support.
To my friends and colleagues – your insights and challenges inspired me to dig deeper and think bigger. Thank you for the journey.
To my readers – thank you for choosing this book. It was written with you in mind, to provide insight and inspiration.

TABLE OF CONTENTS

COPYRIGHT	**1**
DISCLAIMER	**2**
ACKNOWLEDGEMENTS	**4**
TABLE OF CONTENTS	**5**
PREFACE	**7**
ABSTRACT	**13**
MEET THE AUTHOR	**16**
A JOURNEY LIKE NO OTHER	**20**
GRAND ODYSSEY	**26**
PART 1: AWAKENING	**28**
Chapter 1 Where do I start?	29
Chapter 2 See Who You Are	36
LIFE LESSONS - THROUGH THE CAMERA	**51**
PART2: QUEST FOR CLARITY	**55**
Chapter 3 What's going on?	55
UNVARNISHED TRUTHS	**97**
Summaries of Scenarios	97
Chapter 4 "Why Do I Feel Like This?"	102
Chapter 5 "I Know What to Do, or Do I?"	114
PART 3: TOUGH QUESTIONS	**118**
Chapter 6 Answers that count	119
Chapter 7 Who Are You Listening To?	130
Silent Power: Let Your Work Speak	134
PART 4: EMBRACING UNKNOWNS	**138**
Chapter 8 Perception of Loneliness	139

Chapter 9 Technology - Shaping Identity 153
Chapter 10 Digital Nomad – Remote working 157
Chapter 11 Does Religion or Faith Matter? 161

PART 5: GROWTH & TRANSFORMATION 165

Chapter 12 Getting off the Treadmill 166
Chapter 13 Off the Beaten Path Drink, Drugs, Online Dating 179
Chapter 14 "Why Can't I See Anything Ahead of Me?" 186
Chapter 15 Are You Afraid of Your Life? 193
Chapter 16 Do You Trust yourself? 200

PART 6: EXPLORATION 205

Chapter 17 Embracing Infinities 206
Chapter 18 Does Isolation Help? 211
Chapter 19 Coming Up for Air 218

PART 7: EMOTIONAL CROSSROADS 222

Chapter 20 Uncharted Territory 223
Chapter 21 Living Many Lives in One Lifetime 230
Chapter 22 Self-Sufficiency – Road to Recovery 237

PART 8: MOMENTS OF CHANGE 241

Chapter 23 Ticking Clock 242
Chapter 24 Tools for Transformation 245
Chapter 25 What You've Got to Lose? 251
Chapter 26 What You Stand to Gain 255

PART 9: DAYS OF RECKONING 257

Chapter 27 Fear of Unfulfilled Potential 258
Chapter 28 Navigating Love in our Changing World 261

FINAL THOUGHTS 269

APPENDIX A: SONG LIST 271

APPENDIX B: MOVIES 288

APPENDIX C: CULTURAL INFO 292

APPENDIX D: CURATED PLAYLIST 295

PREFACE

We often find ourselves oscillating between best-laid plans and the unexpected. One moment, our ship is steady and predictable: the next, we're blown off course into the unknown, with no script or guidebook. Amid the surf, we ponder our next move and how to adapt.

As disorienting as these moments are, they shape us unimaginably.

These disruptions are familiar, and chances are, you've navigated them well. But perhaps there's another lens to peer through - one that resonates with career transitions, parenting challenges, complex relationships, health issues or the trauma of loss.

The chaos itself is less intriguing than the subtle mental shifts below the surface, those that heighten our awareness. During quiet moments of reflection (often drowned out by noise), we realize that our resilience reservoir is replenished as we endure uncertainties head-on. You understand this already, so let's frame it *differently*. The key is in pausing long enough to hear what lingers beneath the waterline.

Take, for example, the offbeat time signature in "**Take 5**" performed by **The Dave Brubeck Quartet**.

Artist	Title	Scan QR code
The Dave Brubeck Quartet	**Take 5**	

At first, its rhythm seems unpredictable, much like life's unexpected detours. But listen closely: beneath the offbeat, there's an undeniable smoothness - a rhythm you, too, can find during perceived chaos.

This book is for those seeking to explore beyond the obvious - those moments when we need to dig deeper to figure things out. It's not a quick-fix manual; instead, it offers alternative perspectives, using music and film to help reframe how we see things. These layers spark our imagination and cultivate a more fertile, open state of mind.

Now, think about the mindset transition reflected in the iconic song "**Everybody Wants to Rule the World**" performed by **Tears for Fears**.

Artist	**Title**	**Scan QR code**
Tears for Fears	**Everybody wants to rule the world**	

It captures the internal struggle between *ambition* and *acceptance, control* and *surrender*. As you listen, reflect on your own experiences with this universal conflict.
As we strive to gain control over our lives, we often face moments where we must choose between pursuing power or yielding to life's unpredictability.

This tension, highlighted in the song, reminds us that while the desire to rule is universal, true mastery often comes from knowing when to let go.

In contrast, "**Eye in the Sky**" by **The Alan Parsons Project** explores themes of intuition, self-reliance, and the quiet strength of observation.

Artist	Title	Scan QR code
The Alan Parsons Project	Eye in the Sky	

Released in 1982, this song embodies themes of silent authority and calm detachment. The "eye in the sky" symbolizes a higher, unseen force—fate, destiny, or a watchful presence.

The lyrics speak from the perspective of someone who sees through deception and manipulation, confident in their ability to read situations without needing to act impulsively. It reflects a sense of wisdom that comes from understanding and letting things unfold, rather than trying to control them directly. |
This sense of quiet strength, of trusting your instincts and seeing the bigger picture, is captured in one of the most powerful scenes in cinema: ***Scent of a Woman***.

Artist	Title	Scan QR code
Scent of a Woman	*Al Pacino*	

Lieutenant Colonel Frank Slade delivers the unforgettable line - "**There is no prosthetic for an amputated spirit**"- it's a visceral reminder that standing firm in our principles, especially in moments of temptation, defines who we are. This iconic moment resonates because it demonstrates that abandoning our integrity can inflict wounds that no external remedy can heal.

Similarly, **Hans Zimmer's "Now We Are Free"** from Oscar winning **Gladiator** amplifies the emotional weight of cinema's most profound moments, accompanying Maximus's journey of reflection and ultimate triumph.

Movie	Actor	Scan QR code
Gladiator	**Russell Crowe**	

The music rises and falls like the tides of resilience, a reminder that even in the darkest times, we have the strength to rise again.

Bach's Cello Suite No. 1 in G Major begins simply, like the familiar paths we start on. But as the piece deepens, it mirrors life's journey, demanding evolution through obstacles we never anticipated.

Movie	Actor	Scan QR code
Johann Sebastian Bach	***Cello Suite No. 1 in G Major***	

Each note resonates with the weight of experience.

Stillness exists in this turbulence - **Arvo Pärt's "Spiegel im Spiegel"** offers a gentle reminder that space for quiet acceptance is always available, even when we feel lost.

Composer	Composition	Scan QR code
Arvo Pärt	Spiegel im Spiegel	

This book explores the challenges and growth that come when we push beyond easy paths, discovering the rewards of shifting into a higher gear.

Whether you're navigating transitions, dealing with loss, or questioning your identity, this book is your companion for introspection, offering relatable stories, cinematic insights, and the transformative power of music.

Clarity won't come easily.

There are no shortcuts through twists and turns, but in facing them, we discover strength, focus, and, ultimately, ourselves. In uncertainty, it's not about having perfect answers - it's about having the courage to take the first step, knowing that resilience is forged by confronting life's challenges, not by avoiding them.

Trusting your instincts without proof takes a leap of faith, but it's in this space that resilience grows. Much like the quiet strength of **Pat Metheny's "The Truth Will Always Be**," there are moments in life when resilience is built in the spaces between certainty and doubt, in the subtle shifts of trusting yourself over time.

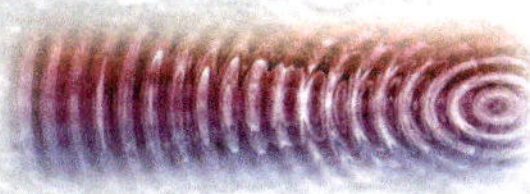

Artist	Composition	Scan QR code
Pat Metheny	The truth will always be	

Running out of road *is not necessarily the* ***end of the tarmac.*** Never underestimate your resilience.

ABSTRACT

Speed is often mistaken for progress, a tempting illusion in a world that prizes shortcuts over substance.

Prepare to be immersed in a synergy of well-known music, film, and vivid stories - thoughtfully woven to enrich *relatable* narratives that spark both interest and imagination.

What if the life we seek lies hidden in paths we fear to tread, unlocked only through trials?

Rooted in *Stoic philosophy*, this book reframes challenges as stepping stones to growth and self-discovery. It champions a resilient way of living, showing how adversity shapes long-term fulfilment through meaningful experiences.

It doesn't simply teach endurance; it inspires the ambition to achieve what once seemed unattainable. It is also an exploration of subtler truths, illuminated through music, film, and provocative stories.

These aren't surface-level parables. They are reflections crafted to challenge and inspire. In a world obsessed with *instant gratification*, this book offers refreshing philosophical reminders and Stoic wisdom that teaches true joy isn't found in quick wins or external validation but in the steady, deliberate pursuit of a life well-lived.

"Never trade quiet, steady effort to craft the meaningful for fleeting applause or hollow victories"

Perseverance, forged in adversity's fire, makes the struggle of hard work deeply meaningful. Adversity isn't a detour from greatness. Take Beethoven's *Symphony No. 9*, a piece so luminous it's tempting to forget it was born from silence.

Composer	Composition	Scan QR code
Ludwig van Beethoven	**Symphony 9 Ode to Joy**	

As Beethoven's world grew quieter, his inner music grew louder. His deafness wasn't just a limitation - it was the canvas against which his masterpiece was painted, reminding us that hardship refines more than it restricts. George Michael offers a modern parallel: his trials, both personal and public, became anthems of resilience for a generation.

Takeaway: Discipline and perseverance form the foundation of success. Challenges serve as catalysts for growth, and through unwavering commitment, especially in times of adversity, ambitions are achieved.

Raising our periscope brings our landscapes into view. Stepping back momentarily from immediate problems allows us to understand how any challenge is part of a greater narrative.

Imagine you're in the kitchen baking a cake, but instead of following the recipe, you decide to skip a few steps and just throw everything into the oven - no mixing, no measuring. Thirty

minutes later, you're faced with something resembling an abstract art piece rather than a dessert. Shortcuts seem clever and timesaving, but the results are less cake and more confusion.

Stoicism advocates for appreciating each step in the process, even if it means stirring the batter, waiting for it to rise, and occasionally burning a few cakes in the process. The real wisdom and growth emerge from the journey itself, not from seeking shortcuts or instant results.

While elbow-deep in flour and frustration, it's easy to lose sight of the bigger picture. But with a step back, you realize that every misstep, every overbaked corner, is part of a larger narrative - perhaps one of becoming a master baker, or at the very least, learning how not to set the kitchen ablaze like Robin Williams in the timeless classic family comedy **Mrs. Doubtfire.** Embracing Stoic principles means understanding that the real prize isn't the perfect cake, but one's perseverance, the laughs at your culinary disasters, and the lessons learned in the process. Ultimately, commit to doing things properly. It matters, even if your delicious cake ends up slightly lopsided!

Artist	**Song**	**Scan QR code**
Bill Withers	**Lovely Day**	

Bill Withers' song ***Lovely Day*** reminds us that even in moments of frustration, real rewards lie in embracing the process with positivity, finding joy in the journey rather than just the outcome.

MEET THE AUTHOR

Life, much like music is a symphony. Multi-layered, improvisational, and deeply personal. For me, music has never been just a passion; it's been a lens through which I've interpreted the world. It's carried me through the highs and lows of my journey - whether exploring distant lands, navigating personal challenges, or finding meaning in quiet moments. Music isn't merely a soundtrack; it's a bridge, a teacher, and a companion. My life feels like Miles Davis' *Kind of Blue* - a masterclass in improvisation, subtlety, and depth.

Musician	Composition	Scan QR code
Miles Davis	*Kind of Blue*	

From the relentless demands of tech finance to the emotional peaks and valleys of marriage, and the bittersweet lessons of loss, I've come to see resilience not as a lofty concept but as a lived truth. It's the quiet strength we uncover when family, friends, and even strangers remind us to listen to their voices, their stories, and the wisdom they offer. Listening, I've found, isn't just a skill; it's an act of connection that builds bridges of empathy and trust. This reverence for others' stories underpins everything I do, including this book. Travel has also shaped my outlook, teaching me that no matter where we are - bustling cities or tucked-away places - stories connect us.

Composer	Composition	Scan QR code
Claude Debussy	Claire de Lune	

Cue Debussy's *Clair de Lune* – it whispers life's quieter moments, teaching us to appreciate the subtle beauty often overlooked. Similarly, the Dave Brubeck Quartet's *Take Five* reminds me that even in life's unexpected detours, there's harmony to be found if we have the patience to seek it. Generosity has been a guiding principle in my life. I believe success means little if it doesn't uplift others. Whether supporting worthy causes, mentoring others, or simply being present when someone has a need, I've found that giving enriches both the giver and the receiver. These values anchor my life - and this book. I've always had a love for creation, whether experimenting with new recipes (recently mastering Beef Wellington), painting the oil portraits that adorn my walls, or capturing fleeting moments with my Leica camera. Music and sound are no different.

Musician	Composition	Scan QR code
Anne Sophie Mutter	***D Minor Op. 47. Allegro moderato***	

It's astonishing how Sebelius symphonies resonate with trials and tribulations of life. Elton John's *Philadelphia Freedom* strikes a perfect balance between structure and spontaneity - reminds me how freedom and discipline work hand in hand to create something extraordinary.

Artist	Song	Scan QR code
Elton John	**Philadelphia Freedom**	

As an audiophile, I pursued the highest fidelity in sound, crafting bespoke turntable setups and audio systems designed to reveal even the faintest nuances of a recording. This commitment to precision extended into my passion for engineering, exemplified by the transformation of my Porsche 993. I upgraded its Varioram engine from a 3.6 to a 3.8, with new valves, a custom vacuum-controlled intake system, equal-length headers, custom cams, and twin wideband Lambda sensors. The Bosch ECU was replaced with a Motec M800 engine management system, a meticulously re-engineered chassis, progressive-rate springs, turbo-specification brakes, every modification executed with purpose and understanding. It was never about ostentation; it was about honoring the art of engineering and pushing the boundaries of performance with a craftsman's attention to detail. It was a labour of love - a complex project that reflected my nature to delve deeply into anything I undertake. A enjoyable learning curve.

Gloria Gaynor's *I Will Survive* is such a timeless anthem.

Movie	Actor	Scan QR code
Gloria Gaynor	***I will survive***	

Meanwhile, Pat Metheny's *Always and Forever* captures the quiet perseverance of resilience, and his *Passaggio Per Il Paradiso* evokes the clarity and peace we find after enduring life's trials.

Musician	Composition	Scan QR code
Pat Metheny	**Always and forever**	

Each chapter of this book weaves together personal stories, cultural touchpoints, and music that has shaped my perspective.

Music isn't just an accompaniment - it's a mentor, offering lessons in creativity, resilience, and the quiet strength needed to craft a meaningful life.

Whether it's the quiet elegance of *Clair de Lune,* the improvisational brilliance of *Kind of Blue,* or the triumphant defiance of *I Will Survive,* these melodies have guided me, and I hope they will inspire you as well.

Finally, I invite you to explore the *No Short Cuts* playlist, a curated collection of masterpieces like Led Zeppelin's *Stairway to Heaven.*

Band	Song	Scan QR code
Led Zeppelin	**Stairway to Heaven**	

The playlist isn't just music - it's an invitation to rediscover.

Artists	Compositions	Scan QR code
Various	**Curated Playlist**	

A JOURNEY LIKE NO OTHER

What does it really mean to thrive, not just survive? As I've walked (and sometimes run) this path, I've learned that life's greatest challenges aren't roadblocks - they're what

help us find the deepest, most fulfilling parts of ourselves. We all choose our own pace, but no matter how we move forward, one thing becomes clear: life is so much more than just a series of events—it's a personal project, and it's messy, complex, and completely worth the effort.

We can't just dream about what we want in life; we must act. Ambitions don't transform into meaningful achievements unless they're tied to discipline, courage, and resilience. When things swing too far off balance, turbulence naturally follows, and sometimes it feels like we're constantly swimming against the tide. But these moments, as hard as they are, are where the real growth happens.

This journey is about learning how to look beyond the obvious and trust your instincts - while knowing that it also takes discipline and perseverance to turn dreams into reality. Ambitions matter, but they're not enough on their own. Reaching the best version of yourself isn't impossible, but it takes a deep commitment.

In this book, you'll find stories, music, and films that have all helped me explore what it means to really live. These genuine experiences, philosophical reflections, and cultural touchpoints help paint a clearer picture of what it means to be human. There are no quick fixes to a meaningful life—every step, every challenge, adds depth to your journey. While no one can guarantee achievements, you can always shift the path you're on.

Take **Beethoven's *Symphony No. 5***. Its powerful notes capture the feeling of life's unexpected knocks - the kind that come when you least expect them.

Band	Song	Scan QR code
Ludwig van Beethoven	***Symphony no.5***	

Those famous four notes symbolize fate itself, reminding us that we must face life's obstacles with courage. Through persistence, we can turn struggle into victory, just like the symphony's triumphant progression.

Just like Beethoven's symphony teaches us to face challenges head-on, Emma's journey (page 71), shows how we must confront our struggles to find growth.

As we continue this journey together, you'll see that the most significant moments in life often happen when we resist shortcuts and dive fully into the process—embracing both the highs and the lows.

Holst's *Jupiter, the Bringer of Jollity* celebrates the joy that comes from being open to life's uncertainties.

Band	Song	Scan QR code
Gustav Holst	***Jupiter, the Bringer of Jollity***	

Every time I hear it, the violin crescendo is like a explosion of energy that never fades.

Holst's melody reminds me of the joy and growth that come from embracing life's winding paths.

Along the way, we'll also explore stories like Emma's, where she rediscovers herself after feeling stuck, and Jake and Mia, who navigate the tricky world of love in the digital age—where words can sometimes be replaced by emojis! These stories are real, not just lessons from a distance. They reflect the struggles and triumphs that shape us, helping you see your own journey through their experiences. Even if their stories don't match your own, sharing these experiences creates valuable context. It's through this lens that *No Shortcuts* offers practical insights, paired with music, to help you see the bigger picture. Whether you're facing a career change, navigating relationships, studying, running a business, or simply searching for meaning, this book offers light-hearted but

insightful ways to look at life with fresh eyes—even if you think you've already figured it all out.

There's plenty of fun to be had, but don't worry—we won't lose sight of the important stuff.

Music runs throughout these pages, helping bring the stories to life and giving you the chance to reflect on your own experiences. This approach offers a more artistic, creative alternative to the typical self-help book. The stories are real, relatable, and told in simple terms so you can easily apply them to your own life.

You'll find references to cultural touchpoints - from

The Shawshank Redemption to **Shirley Bassey's "I Am What I Am"** - adding emotional depth to these stories. You'll also find ancient wisdom, especially from Stoicism, offering practical advice on how to handle life's challenges with resilience and purpose.

Each chapter wraps up with **reflections, calls to action,** or **tips** to enhance your experience.

We shall dive into why shortcuts only lead to short-term gains, and how the real value comes from investing time and energy into the tough challenges. Real satisfaction rarely comes from the easy route - unless you're unusually lucky or privileged.

Philosophical Reflections

This book draws on ancient wisdom, particularly Stoicism, offering practical insights on how to face life's challenges with resilience and purpose.

Practical Takeaways

Each chapter ends with calls to action, reflections, or tips to help you navigate your journey with clarity and purpose.

Grind it out, *without complaint*, and see how each challenge becomes part of your story. **Your very own symphony.**

Rewards await those willing to put in the time and effort.

Taoist philosophy emphasizes the concept of **Wu Wei**, or "effortless action."

Rather than fighting against the natural flow of events, Taoism teaches us to align with the rhythms of life.

Just as a river flows effortlessly toward its destination, we, too, can find strength by allowing life to unfold naturally.

By trusting the process and adapting to the present moment, we discover that struggle is not always necessary for growth; sometimes, surrendering to the journey allows us to reach new heights.

Media

Ludovico Einaudi "Experience" complement the Taoist concept of going with the flow and finding balance in life's journey.

Band	Song	Scan QR code
Ludovico Einaudi	***Experience***	

GRAND ODYSSEY

No GPS. No kind stranger waving you in the right direction. And absolutely no tea break to mull it all over. Life doesn't hand you a neat map with a "You Are Here" sticker, yet every day, golden opportunities are quietly, almost mischievously, hiding in plain sight. The real question is: *Are you paying attention?*

Shortcuts, like microwaved soufflés, promise quick satisfaction but rarely deliver substance. Carly Simon's *"Nobody Does It Better"* slyly reminds us that true excellence is custom-built—you, my friend, are the architect.

Band	Song	Scan QR code
Carly Simon	***Nobody does it better***	

Think about it: achieving your best self isn't a matter of perfection—it's about resilience, that unglamorous, gritty consistency that keeps you moving forward, one step at a time. Stability isn't flashy, but it's the unsung hero of measurable progress.

But let's not romanticize the slog. Some days feel like marching through quicksand, armed with little more than blind faith and yesterday's stale coffee. And that's okay. The secret lies in embracing the peculiar beauty of the struggle—because no one else is equipped to write your story quite like you.

When life feels particularly foggy, music has a way of cutting through the haze. Ludovico Einaudi's *"Nuvole Bianche"* is the perfect companion for these moments. Its quiet strength doesn't shout solutions; it whispers, "Breathe. Trust. Keep going."

And for those days when it's tempting to throw in the towel—or at least sit on it—Roxy Music's *"Don't Stop the Dance"* reminds us that the rhythm of life marches on. You don't need to know all the moves; you just need to stay in the groove.

Band	Song	Scan QR code
Roxy Music	**Don't stop the dance**	

Here's another thing: stop blaming your friends. They're not mind readers, nor are they your guardians. Yes, having a supportive network is wonderful, but it's not their job to carry you or to intuit every nuance of your life. Leaning on them too much turns support into strain. Friendship works best when it's reciprocal—not when it feels like a part-time job.

So where do you begin? With courage—sometimes shaky, often reluctant, but courage, nonetheless. With action, even if it's clumsy at first. And with the unshakable belief that, despite the noise, the setbacks, and the self-doubt, you're uniquely equipped for this journey.

Because at the end of the day, Carly was right: nobody does it better than you.

PART 1: AWAKENING

This section explores self-discovery, identity, and personal purpose

Chapter 1 **Where Do I Start?**

Introducing foundational themes of reflection, resilience, and personal growth..

A leap of Faith

Chapter 2 **See Who You Are**

Delving into the facets of self-awareness and the journey toward authenticity.

Connecting Identity for purpose
Tempering Resilience
Self-Discovery
Embracing Change
Personal Compass
Life lessons through the camera

Chapter 1

Where do I start?

Picture this: a grand theatrical performance. The lights dim, the audience holds its breath, and the curtain rises to the crescendo of a drum roll. It's the kind of entrance you'd imagine for royalty. But for the rest of us? Our journeys often begin with far less spectacle - more like fumbling with a flashlight in the dark, hoping the batteries hold out.

Starting anything new is more than a physical act. It's the moment you trade the comfort of familiarity for the vast, unnerving terrain of possibility. It's a quiet step forward, brimming with potential. Yet, all too often, the poverty of low expectations pins us in place, whispering that the unknown isn't worth the risk.

Whether it's a career pivot, a bold creative endeavour, or even reshaping your relationships, the first step takes courage - especially when the path ahead is shrouded in uncertainty. Ironically, it's that very uncertainty that makes the journey worthwhile. Without it, growth would be as thrilling as watching paint dry.

I remember a friend confiding in me during a particularly bleak season of his life. Maybe you've got a friend like that or perhaps it's you. Trapped in routine, stuck in self-doubt, longing for an undecided change but unsure where to start. If that sounds familiar, you're not alone.

After months of hesitation, he finally took one small step: he enrolled in a class aligned with his passion, not knowing where it might lead. It wasn't a grand gesture, but that single act became the hinge upon which his life turned. What followed was a series of deliberate choices that opened doors he didn't even know existed.

As he shared his story, I couldn't help but think of *California Dreamin'* by The Mamas & the Papas:

Artist	**Title**	**Scan QR code**
Mamas and papas	***California dreaming***	

You'll notice I'm weaving music into these moments. Why? Because music is one of life's universal translators. A single song can encapsulate emotions we struggle to put into words, and it has a way of turning personal experiences into shared ones. These tracks are here to do just that - to resonate with you, to spark reflection, and maybe even inspire your next step.

This song's imagery of longing for warmth while being stuck in the cold captured my friend's situation perfectly. He yearned for something more, for a life beyond the icy grip of routine. His first step was a reminder that we all endure our own winters, waiting for the courage to move toward the flowers of spring we all deserve.

Sometimes, we live lives that feel out of sync with our values - like governing politically *left* when you campaigned *right*. This dissonance, though uncomfortable, holds a mirror to the adjustments we all need to make. To start your plan, act from a place of truth. Makes more sense to align your actions with your core principles. Hold onto your vision, but don't cling so tightly that you refuse to adapt. True growth is a tango between ambition and practicality, like balancing visionary ideals with grounded action. Cloud Coocoo land has no place here.

This isn't about shortcuts; there are none. It's about answering the question, *"Where do I start?"* That quiet nudge is life's way of reminding us to act, even when the road ahead feels murky.

For me, this moment is encapsulated by *Take On Me* by A-ha:

Artist	**Title**	**Scan QR code**
A-ha	**Take On Me**	

The song's electric energy is the perfect anthem for seizing the moment. Its tempo, like the heartbeat of determination, captures the urgency of breaking free from hesitation and leaping into the unknown. It's that leap—half courage, half hope - that transforms possibilities into realities.

Every great journey begins not with knowing every answer but with trusting the process. Before taking your first step, pause. Reflect. Much like Erik Satie's *Gymnopédie No. 1*, the beginning of any journey is grounded in stillness:

Artist	Title	Scan QR code
Erik Satie	Gymnopédie No. 1	

Its serene melody invites introspection, offering clarity as we align our heart and mind. It's a gentle reminder that the answers we seek often lie within us, waiting for the noise to subside.

But stillness isn't always enough. Sometimes, life demands resilience. Freddie Hubbard's *Little Sunflower* plays like a soulful anthem for those moments:

Artist	Title	Scan QR code
Freddie Hubbard	Little Sunflower	

Its melody is both soothing and filled with quiet strength, much like the sunflower turning toward the sun. It teaches us to seek light even in life's shadows, trusting that growth comes in its own time. Contrast this with Shirley Bassey's *Where Do I Begin?*, a hauntingly beautiful ballad that mirrors the vulnerability of new beginnings:

Artist	Title	Scan QR code
Shirley Bassey	Where do I begin	

Its slow build reflects the hesitant yet powerful process of starting, showing us that every note of uncertainty adds to the symphony of progress.

Finally, *Diary of Dreams* by Stavros Lantsias invites us into moments of solitude and reflection:

Artist	Title	Scan QR code
Stavros Lantsias	Diary of Dreams	

Its delicate piano melody is a fitting soundtrack for embracing vulnerability, while Pat Metheny's *Passaggio Per Il Paradiso* reminds us that even in darkness, each step brings us closer to the light:

Artist	Title	Scan QR code
Pat Metheny	Passaggio per il Paradiso	

Its uplifting tones are a testament to the hope that fuels our journeys forward.

Takeaways

Start Now: *The perfect moment is often a myth.* Begin anyway.

Define Your "Why": Ambition without clarity is like a ship without a rudder.

Embrace Setbacks: They're not roadblocks; they're *steppingstones.*

Find Inspiration: Whether it's mentors, music or perhaps dip your toe into unusual experiences, let them fuel you.

Celebrate Progress: No step is too small. Acknowledge your wins.

A Leap of Faith

The truth is, you don't need all the answers to get going - just the metal to take that crucial first step.

Proof

- Every footprint you leave behind is undeniable evidence that you're moving forward, even if it does not feel so.

- We often try to convince ourselves that clarity must come before action. But here's the paradox: the answers we seek usually appear only after we begin.

- There's no universal formula or foolproof set of instructions waiting for you.

The question *"Where do I start?"* isn't something others can answer - it's already embedded within you, rooted in your unique blend of experiences, aspirations, and fears. Yes, it might sound fluffy, but the real work begins when you start unravelling it. It's less about knowing the exact way forward and more about trusting yourself - and relying less on those you lean on for guidance.

Chapter 2

See Who You Are

Knowing yourself. In the quest for a meaningful and purposeful life, this chapter begins with a profound yet often overlooked concept: self-awareness. To embark on this journey, we must first look inward to truly see who we are.

Imagine walking into a room filled with mirrors, each one reflecting not just your face but your choices, dreams, and doubts. For some, it's a glimpse of potential; for others, it's a reminder of what's been left undone. In truth, most of us avoid this room entirely. Why? Because seeing ourselves clearly can be unsettling.

In a world filled with distractions and external influences, it's easy to lose sight of our authentic selves. We wear masks to fit in, conform to societal expectations, and often overlook our own desires and values. But "See Who You Are" beckons us to peel back those layers, dig beneath the surface, and confront the person staring back at us in the mirror.

Self-awareness is the foundation of a meaningful life, yet it's often treated like flossing - important, sure, but easy to skip. To truly know who we are, we must take an unflinching look in that metaphorical mirror, confronting not just our strengths but also the vulnerabilities we'd rather keep hidden.

The late Michael Jackson captured this idea aptly in *Man in the Mirror*:

Artist	Title	Scan QR code
Michael Jackson	Man in the mirror	

His lyrics, "I'm starting with the man in the mirror, I'm asking him to change his ways," remind us that transformation begins within. The mirror reflects both what we celebrate and what we avoid, and it's in this confrontation that growth begins.

Think of it as emotional spring cleaning: uncomfortable, messy, but ultimately liberating. The mirror doesn't lie - it shows us the parts of ourselves we've been avoiding, and it's only when we confront those truths that we can move forward.

Peeling Back the Layers

We live in a world that thrives on distractions. Social media, work obligations, and the endless pursuit of "busy" provide convenient excuses to sidestep introspection. Instead, we don masks—versions of ourselves curated to meet expectations, fit in, or simply keep the peace. But what happens when the mask doesn't fit anymore?

Let It Be by The Beatles offers timeless wisdom for this journey:

Artist	Title	Scan QR code
The Beetles	Let it be	

"When I find myself in times of trouble, Mother Mary comes to me, speaking words of wisdom, let it be." These words remind us that self-awareness isn't about perfection; it's about acceptance.

The Influence of Culture

Our sense of self isn't formed in a vacuum. Cultural expectations - whether from family, society, or heritage - shape how we view ourselves. In Eastern cultures, identity often revolves around community and family roles, while Western societies place a heavier emphasis on individualism. For those navigating multiple cultural identities, the challenge lies in balancing these sometimes-conflicting influences.

A mixed-heritage friend once described her identity as "a Venn diagram where the circles never quite meet." For her, self-awareness meant honouring both the traditions she grew up with and the personal values she'd forged as an adult. It's a balancing act, but one that's worth the effort. Recognizing these influences is the first step toward uncovering your authentic self.

Let's explore the tools and techniques for cultivating self-awareness, drawing from the wisdom of psychologists, philosophers, and individuals who have embarked on their own journeys of self-discovery.

Seeing who we are is not a selfish endeavour, but a prerequisite for building meaningful relationships, pursuing fulfilling careers, and making a positive impact on the world.

As we delve deeper into the exploration of self-awareness, embrace the discomfort that may arise as you confront your own truths, for it is through this discomfort that we learn, evolve, and ultimately become more authentic versions of ourselves.

Let's begin this chapter with an open mind, ready to understand ourselves better. By gaining self-awareness, we can find the clarity and purpose needed to walk through complexities of life in a mode that feels right.

Connecting Identity for Purpose

Your identity and purpose are two sides of the same coin, intricately connected. The more you understand yourself - your passions, strengths, and values—the clearer your sense of purpose becomes.

And in turn, as you pursue what gives you meaning, you uncover deeper layers of who you are. It's not about having all the answers today; sometimes, purpose is as simple as getting through a challenging moment. But with each step, the pieces of your life's puzzle fall into place. Stay open, because both you and your purpose are evolving together.

Tempering Resilience: Amputated Spirits

In the journey of life, there are battles we fight that leave scars unseen by the world - wounds that cut deeper than any physical injury. These are the wounds inflicted on our spirit when we compromise our integrity, betray our values, or let fear dictate our choices. As Lieutenant Colonel Frank Slade powerfully asserts in ***Scent of a Woman***, "There is no prosthetic for an amputated spirit." No external fix, no material compensation can restore a spirit that has been

broken by the choices we regret or the principles we've abandoned.

Artist	Title	Scan QR code
Scent of a Woman	Al Pacino	

Our spirit, our inner self, is the core of who we are.
It's what drives us, gives us purpose, and keeps us moving forward even when the world seems to conspire against us.

When life's challenges threaten to overwhelm us, we must remember that resilience isn't about never falling - it's about having the courage to rise again and continue the dance. In the face of adversity, when you get tangled up, you don't stop - you tango on. This is the dance of life, where resilience and integrity guide our steps, ensuring that our spirit remains whole and vibrant.

Cue *Spandau Ballet's "True."*

Artist	Title	Scan QR code
Spandau Ballet	True	

Its message of honesty and vulnerability resonates. Living authentically means recognizing when we've veered off course and having the courage to realign. It no small feat in a world that often rewards conformity over authenticity. But as *True* reminds us, being honest with yourself is the ultimate act of self-respect.

Self-Discovery

Let's strip this back to basics. This isn't about "fixing" anything - it's about clarity. Unclogging a pipeline because time, sediment accumulates - external expectations, misguided influences, even our own distractions. The water's still there, but its flow impeded until we clear the way. A metaphor for your self-discovery. It's not about adding something new; it's about removing what doesn't

belong. And here's the thing: sometimes, it's not just sediment clogging the flow – it is ballast weighing us down like a hot air balloon impeded by unnecessary weight, limiting altitude. Whether it's old grudges, toxic influences, or self-imposed limitations, holding onto them keeps you tethered. The moment you let go, you rise. And as you rise, the air gets clearer. The view gets better.

Moving on

Self-discovery isn't about adding layers; it's about peeling them back to find what's already there - like subtle things: outdated beliefs, habits, and, yes, the people who quietly drain the air from your room. Do not try to change anyone, but you can change negative influence. Reclaim your space -unburdened and unapologetially Lady Gaga's *Born This Way* captures this perfectly:

Artist	Title	Scan QR code
Lady Gaga	Born this way	

This isn't just a celebration of individuality; it's a reminder that authenticity is about stripping back—not performing. "I'm on the right track, baby, I was born this way," isn't a boast—it's a declaration of freedom. It's about saying no to the sediment, the ballast, and the oxygen thieves. It's about breathing deeply and soaring higher.

Your Personal Compass

Think of self-awareness as your compass. It's not showy, but it's reliable. It doesn't give you a detailed map, but it keeps you heading in the right direction. And let's be honest: sometimes we ignore it. We drift, take wrong turns, and blame the currents. But the compass is still there, waiting for us to look down and recalibrate.

Here's the beauty of it: even detours have their value. They remind us to pause and ask, "What's really important? What's weighing me down? What am I holding onto that no longer serves me?" Releasing the ballast doesn't mean abandoning everything—it means letting go of what keeps you from rising.

Life's detours might frustrate us, but they're often where the best lessons hide. Even when the road feels rocky, the compass gently reminds us: adjust your course, keep moving, and trust the journey.

Final Words

Maybe self-discovery isn't about finding yourself - it's about clearing the way for who you've always been. It's about releasing the ballast, clearing the sediment, and making room for your authentic self to rise. It's not about perfection or even certainty. It's about embracing the raw, unpolished, and sometimes uncomfortable truth of who you are.

This journey isn't tidy, but it's honest. It's not easy, but it's freeing. And the best part? You're the one holding the compass, the map, and the keys to the treasure chest. So, take a deep breath, release what's weighing you down, and trust that with each step, you're getting closer to the clearest, truest version of yourself.

Embracing Change

Rolling with the Punches

Here's the thing: life is full of surprises. Sometimes, they're the good kind - like finding money in your winter coat or down the sofa. Other times, they're more like realizing that your favorite jeans have shrunk (and by "shrunk," I mean you've maybe indulged in one too many slices of pizza). The point is, life changes, and so do you. And that's okay.

Your values and priorities aren't carved in stone - they're more like your favorite playlist that evolves over time. What was once your favourite might not hit the same spot anymore. So, when you do these check-ins, don't be surprised if you find that what mattered to you a few years ago doesn't hold the same weight now.

Embrace change - after all, no one wants to be stuck replaying the same track over and over.

Change brings growth, and variety keeps life interesting.

Bridging gaps

Recognizing where you're out of sync with your values is the first step toward real change. But awareness alone isn't enough; *it's what you do next that counts.*

The goal is to bring your actions into harmony with your values, **to close the gap** between who you are and how you're living. This might mean setting **firmer boundaries** at work so that you can spend more time with your family. It could involve making a commitment to *healthier eating* and *regular exercise* if you've been neglecting your well-being.

or...

Maybe it's about recalibrating your personal goals to better reflect what truly matters to you now, not just what you thought you wanted years ago. These adjustments don't have to be drastic, but they do need to be intentional.

Small, consistent changes can lead to significant shifts over time. It's about making sure that your daily actions - *no matter how small* - are a **true reflection** of your deepest values.

Seeking Outside Perspective

Ever feel too close to a situation to see it clearly?

That's where the perspectives of trusted friends, mentors, or even a therapist become invaluable.

These people offer insights you might have overlooked, helping you recognize areas where you're out of alignment.

They challenge you to think differently, move beyond your comfort zone, and take authentic steps forward.

Stay ***open*** *to what you may find.*

A relatable soundtrack.

Artist	Title	Scan QR code
Coldplay	Talk	

- **Welcome feedback**, *even when it stings*
- **Set pride aside** - *it shouldn't hold back your growth*

Think of someone whose perspective you trust.
What might they see that you don't?

Self-Compassion

Beating yourself up

Now, let's touch on self-compassion. Imagine you're trying to learn how to skateboard (why? Because why not!). On your first attempt gliding gracefully will not happen so we expect to be way off balance and you're probably going to look a little silly whilst doing it. Laugh it off and give yourself the same consideration you would give a friend who is giving a shot to something new.

Remember, self-compassion isn't about letting yourself off the hook for everything.

It's about recognizing that you're human, and sometimes being human means eating an entire bowl of ice cream or a chocolate brownie after a tough day. And you know what? That's okay.

Self-discovery is unpredictable, often resulting in confusion along the way.

But nothing compares to the payoff. Each step leads to growth, and the rewards can transform life in unforesable ways.

Takeaways / Actionable steps

- **Schedule** *Reflection*: Set aside time to reassess your values and ensure you're living your own dream, not someone else's.

- **Embrace** *Change*: Accept that evolving values and identity are natural; change is life's way of keeping things dynamic.

- **Practice** *Self-Compassion*: Mistakes are part of growth. Learn to laugh at them and keep moving forward.

- **Clarify** *Purpose*: Focus on what gives you meaning today, even if it's just getting through Monday.

- **Journal** *Regularly*: Capture insights and reflections - a great way to track your personal growth.

- **Reach Out:** *Talk* to trusted friends for perspective or a good laugh.

- **Celebrate** *Progress*: Acknowledge every step forward - celebrate your wins, big or small.

- **Regular** *Check-ins*:
  Make Reflection a Habit.

  Keep it light, fun, and enjoy the ride – cake (optional), ***but highly recommended!***

Humour is so vital

Sing in the shower (embrace the embarrassment)

Dance to corny pop music and remember: life's too short to take it all too seriously.

LIFE LESSONS - THROUGH THE CAMERA

Cinema, like literature, is more than entertainment; it's a powerful mirror reflecting the complexities of the human experience.

Through the stories told on screen, we encounter the struggles, triumphs, and profound moments that shape who we are.

The films selected in this chapter aren't just celebrated for their artistry; they resonate deeply because they capture **real-life emotions, historical contexts, and universal truths**.

What makes these films particularly compelling is their **authenticity**. Even in comedies, we recognize situations that mirror our own lives, drawing us in through relatable moments that feel genuine.
Directors skillfully tap into these connections, weaving in references to real-world scenarios—sometimes subtle, sometimes overt - that demand our attention.
The magic lies in how they twist these familiar narratives, offering fresh perspectives through drama, adventure, comedy, or even science fiction.
This blend of realism and creative reimagining gives film its unique power to captivate.

As we explore these cinematic stories, we uncover lessons that echo the core themes of this book. Each film provides **timeless wisdom** that doesn't just entertain but invites us to reflect on our own journeys toward meaning and fulfillment.

The Shawshank Redemption

The Power of Hope

Andy Dufresne's unyielding hope reminds us that true resilience isn't about avoiding hardship, but about believing in a better future, even in the darkest times (see Chapter 4). How does hope shape the way you face your own challenges?

Dead Poets Society

Seize the Day

John Keating's message of "Carpe Diem" inspires us to break free from societal constraints and live authentically. How might you seize the day and live more in alignment with your values (see Chapter 5)?

A Beautiful Mind

Love and Resilience

John Nash's battle with schizophrenia shows us that resilience isn't a solo endeavour; it's strengthened by the love and support of others (see Chapter 6). Who in your life provides the support that helps you persevere?

The Pursuit of Happiness

Relentless Perseverance

Chris Gardner's journey reminds us that success comes not from avoiding adversity but from pushing through it (see Chapter 4). When have you persisted against the odds, and what did you learn from the experience?

Rocky

The Underdog's Triumph

Rocky Balboa teaches us that real victory lies not in winning but in proving to ourselves that we can go the distance (see Chapter 3). How are you pushing yourself to go further than you ever thought possible?

Good Will Hunting

Self-Discovery

Will Hunting's journey of self-awareness reminds us of the power of mentorship and confronting our fears (see Chapter 8). What fears are holding you back, and who can help you face them?

Forrest Gump

Living Authentically

Forrest Gump's simple, honest approach to life shows us that authenticity leads to true fulfilment (see Chapter 2). What would happen if you lived with Forrest's sense of integrity and resilience?

The Matrix

Choosing Truth Over Comfort

Neo's choice to face the harsh truths of reality mirrors the book's theme of embracing self-awareness (see Chapter 7). Are you ready to challenge the comfortable illusions in your own life?

The Godfather

Power and Moral Dilemmas

Michael Corleone's transformation explores the complex relationship between power, loyalty, and integrity (see Chapter 9). How do your values hold up when tested by external pressures?

It's a Wonderful Life

The Value of Life

George Bailey's realization of his own worth teaches us the profound impact of one life on many (see Chapter 10). How can you start recognizing the value of your own life and its ripple effect on those around you?

The Cinematic Compass

These films, while diverse in their narratives and characters, offer profound insights into the human experience.

As we reflect on these stories, we find that the themes they explore are not confined to the screen; they are the very same challenges, triumphs, and moral dilemmas we face in our own lives.

Can you draw any comparisons with your own life experiences?

PART2: QUEST FOR CLARITY

Chapter 3

What's going on?

A collection of *real-life scenarios* explored.

Scenario 1: Childhood – *Where Did the Seasons Go?*

Scenario 2: Sarah – *Career Crossroads*

Scenario 3: David and Sarah – *Midlife Crossroads*

Scenario 4: Emma and Tom – *Growth vs. Tradition*

Scenario 5: Jake and Mia – *Love in the Digital Age*

Scenario 6: Evelyn & Henry – *Lifetime of Love & Loss*

Scenario 7: Susan – *The Empty Nest*

Scenario 8: Mark – *Fastlane*

Explore each scenario to uncover unique lessons on life's pivotal moments

Scenario 1

Childhood - Where did the seasons go?

The story of childhood has changed. There was a time when growing up meant running outside until dusk, building hideouts from branches, and turning any patch of grass into a universe of endless adventure doing cartwheels. Today, children's playgrounds have shifted into the digital realm, where imagination is guided by algorithms and friendships are mediated through screens. The world has changed, and with it, childhood has become something different from the one many of us knew.

Television, once a shared experience with family, has become a more isolated, on-demand activity. We grew up with only a handful of TV channels, but each show felt like an event - ***Scooby-Doo, Batman, The Jetsons***, and ***Looney Tunes*** filled our imaginations with ideas. These moments were shared with friends or family, bringing us together. Today, with endless channels and streaming options, television has become a solitary escape, another way to *disconnect* from the world rather than *connect* with it.

The music we grew up with was different, too. Pink Floyd's ***Another Brick in the Wall*** captures the increasing isolation today's kids face - absorbing endless content yet building digital walls that separate them from the outside world.

Artist	Title	Scan QR code
Pink Floyd	**Brick in the Wall**	

Terry Jacks' "Seasons in the Sun" echoes the simplicity and joy of childhood that many of today's children might never experience, as their lives become more about screens and less about sunlit adventures.

Artist	Title	Scan QR code
Terry Jacks	Seasons in the Sun	

However, it's important to remember that *not all children* are experiencing childhood this way. Many parents today are *proactive* in ensuring their kids have well-rounded experiences. They're enrolling their children in music lessons, encouraging them to learn instruments, join sports teams, and even participate in organizations like army cadets or engage in creative activities like theatre or art. Some children are even deeply involved in fundraising for charitable causes, demonstrating a maturity and responsibility beyond their years. These efforts highlight that not all childhoods are dominated by screens or isolation. There are many who thrive, showcasing balance, creativity, and leadership at a young age.

At the same time, parents are under immense pressure to prepare their children for a fast-changing, technology-driven future. They know that the world their children will enter as adults is one shaped by technological advancement and innovation. Steering children toward the right skills and qualifications is a priority. Ensuring they graduate with not only good academic credentials but also the digital literacy needed for tomorrow's job market is critical—and it's not easy. This responsibility weighs heavily on many parents, both financially and emotionally. From coding classes to extracurricular activities, the investment is significant. The future feels uncertain, and parents walk a fine line between encouraging well-rounded growth and ensuring their children are not left behind in the race for technological competency.

Today's children face a new set of pressures. Social media, relationships, and adult realities confront them earlier than ever. The world has sped up, and kids are leaving childhood behind faster than previous generations. The question remains: how does this change affect the values we carry into adulthood? And how do we find clarity in a world that looks so different from the one we imagined as children?

Takeaway

It's not about rejecting technology or condemning progress but using roadblocks. It's about remembering what childhood was meant to be: *joy, imagination, and discovery.*

How can we help today's children find the ***balance*** between ***innovation*** and ***imagination***?

So, to the children growing up today: let your ***seasons have sun***, let your ***friendships be real***, and let your lives be as free as the dreams *you once had* as kids!

Scenario 2

Sarah - Career Crossroads

Sarah had always been a force to be reckoned with - a woman whose ambition and drive propelled her to the upper echelons of the corporate world. Her days were a blur of high-stakes meetings, strategic decisions, and accolades that marked her as a rising star in her industry.

The promotions came swiftly, the pay cheques grew larger, and her life seemed to be a model of success.

Yet, as the years passed, something insidious began to creep into her consciousness—a feeling of profound disconnection.

In the stillness of her evenings, when the noise of the day subsided, Sarah found herself grappling with a question that gnawed at the edges of her mind: *"What's going on with my life?"* It wasn't an easy question to confront, for it threatened to unravel the very fabric of her carefully constructed identity.

She had built her life on the foundations of hard work, ambition, and the pursuit of success. But now, those very foundations felt shaky, as if the edifice she had erected was hollow at its core.

The boardrooms, once arenas of exhilaration, now felt suffocating. The thrill of closing a deal no longer sparked the joy it once did. Sarah began to realize that the accolades and promotions, which she had once chased with such fervour, had become mere markers in a race that no longer excited her.

The passion that had once fuelled her ambition was flickering, dimmed by the relentless grind of corporate expectations. Sarah sat in yet another boardroom meeting, her hands clenched under the table. The energy that once fueled her ambition had drained, leaving a hollow ache in its place. Each word from her colleagues felt distant, muffled by the weight of her own thoughts. 'Is this it?' she wondered, her pulse quickening as the walls seemed to close in.

It was the same feeling that *Andy Sachs* wrestled with in *"The Devil Wears Prada"*, where the high-powered, glamorous world of fashion lost its sheen, revealing the emotional and spiritual cost of chasing success on someone else's terms. Like Andy, Sarah was forced to confront a sobering reality: despite the prestige and the outward success, she was no longer fulfilled by the path she was on. The thought of leaving it all behind terrified her.

How does one walk away from the security of a well-paying job, from the prestige of a respected title? The unknown loomed large, a vast and uncharted territory filled with both promise and peril.

Yet, the alternative - continuing down a path that left her feeling empty—was equally daunting.

This wasn't just about a career change. For Sarah, it was a deeper existential shift, where her once-clear dreams of success now seemed more complex, colored by experience and the passage of time. It is a reminder of **Joni Mitchell's *Both Sides, Now*** - a song that captures the bittersweet realization that life's most cherished illusions often evolve as we gain perspective. Like Sarah, the song reflects how time changes not just our ambitions but our understanding of them, making us see the world—and ourselves - with fresh eyes.

Artist	Title	Scan QR code
Joni Mitchel	Both sides now	

She began to explore the possibilities that lay beyond the corporate world. What if she could find work that resonated with her soul, that aligned with her values and passions? The more she entertained the idea, the more she realized that the life she had been living was out of sync with her deepest desires. But she didn't make the decision overnight. It was a slow, deliberate process of disentangling herself from the expectations that had once defined her.

She sought out mentors who had made similar transitions, read books on finding purpose, and even took up journaling to help clarify her thoughts. Each step she took brought her closer to the realization that true success is not measured by titles or pay cheques, but by the sense of fulfilment and alignment with one's true self.

The day Sarah handed in her resignation, she felt both terrified and free. Her hands trembled as she closed her laptop for the last time. The office, once a symbol of achievement, now felt foreign. She stepped outside, the city alive with noise, but inside her, there was a strange calm. She had no idea what was next, but for the first time in years, she was okay with that. 'This is my life,' she thought, 'and it's finally mine to shape.

Fulfillment isn't simply about ticking off achievements; it's about figuring out what really matters to you. Sarah didn't know exactly what the future held, but she knew one thing for sure - she wasn't going to live for anyone else's expectations anymore. Her journey was a lot like Walter Mitty's in ***The Secret Life of Walter Mitty***.

Just like Mitty left the safe and predictable to discover something deeper, Sarah was stepping away from the comfort of what she knew and venturing into the uncharted territories of her own heart.

Walter's journey wasn't just a physical adventure - it was a quest to rediscover his inner world, much like Sarah's. Each step she took was a leap into the unknown, frightening yet liberating, filled with the realization that the most meaningful adventures are often the ones we take within ourselves.

Takeaway

Sarah's story is a powerful testament to the courage it takes to reassess one's path and make a change. It reminds us, much like the characters in *"The Devil Wears Prada"* and *"The Secret Life of Walter Mitty,"* that our careers should be an expression of our passions and values, not just a means to an end. *Joni Mitchell's* hauntingly beautiful *"Both Sides, now"* mirrors Sarah's inner journey—the realization that fulfilment doesn't come from external markers of success, but from alignment with our deepest selves.

The decision to leave behind a life that no longer serves us is not one of failure, but of profound growth and self-discovery.

In choosing to realign her life with her aspirations, Sarah found not just a new career, but a renewed sense of purpose and joy.

How do these movies relate?

Film - *"The Devil Wears Prada"* This film perfectly captures the existential conflict Sarah faces. Like Andy Sachs, Sarah must confront the question of whether her career success is worth the personal cost. The film is relatable for those who have ever questioned the value of their high-powered careers and offers a compelling narrative about choosing personal fulfilment over societal expectations.

Film - *"The Secret Life of Walter Mitty"*: This film exemplifies the transformative journey Sarah embarks upon. Walter Mitty's transition from a routine, safe life to one filled with adventure and self-discovery parallels Sarah's leap into the unknown. Both characters are searching for something deeper than external success.

Music - *"Both Sides, now" by Joni Mitchell*: Mitchell's song beautifully encapsulates Sarah's emotional journey. Its reflective lyrics about life's complexities and changing perspectives resonate with Sarah's evolving understanding of what true success and fulfilment mean. This song invites listeners to introspect as they follow Sarah's transformative path.

Here's how career crossroads was unpacked

Questioning the Path

Sarah finds herself at a turning point, asking, *"What's going on with my life?"* Her career, once fulfilling, no longer brings her joy, marking the beginning of her realization that she's at a crossroads.

Fear of the Unknown

The thought of leaving her established career terrifies Sarah, as she grapples with the security of her prestigious role versus the potential of pursuing something more meaningful. This fear of transitioning into something unfamiliar is a hallmark of a *career crossroads* moment.

Deliberation and Self-Discovery

Sarah's process of slowly disentangling herself from her corporate identity—seeking mentors, journaling, and exploring alternative paths—captures the essence of someone at a career crossroads, weighing the decision to stay in a comfortable but unfulfilling job or step into something more aligned with her passions.

Taking the step

Ultimately, Sarah's journey mirrors the experiences of many at a *career crossroads*, deciding not just to change jobs, but to realign her life with her values, redefining what success means to her.

Her journey is about more than a career switch -it's about existential realignment.

Relationship Rollercoasters

As is the case with any major transitions such as relationships, career changes, getting older, health issues from work stress, or trying to keep up with the digital world, it all seems straightforward at first. Much like putting together IKEA furniture, you start with excitement and a plan, confident it'll all come together seamlessly. But soon enough, you're standing there with leftover screws and wondering where it went wrong. Life's kind of like that—simple in theory, but it's full of unexpected twists and complications. We've all been there in one form or another.

When relationships begin, we feel a palpable lift of enthusiasm, what seems like unbridled energy, both of you moving in perfect harmony. The funny things are, one does not seem to try very hard - seems to come so naturally – very little wasted energy, especially when you both decide to retire for the evening!

But as time passes, you quickly realize the steps get more intricate. Maintaining that connection required constant adjustment, growth, and the courage to face some difficult truths. Whether you're young or old, male or female, you know that the honeymoon period is rarely infinite – Goes without saying - demands work and lots of compromise.

And not just relationships.

Careers, too, start off with a clear trajectory, but as the years go by, many of us face the question, "Is this really where I want to be?" Add to that the toll of work stress, health concerns creeping up, or just feeling like you're running out of steam—suddenly, things aren't as simple as they once seemed.

Then there's the digital world, where younger generations navigate an endless stream of information, trying to find their identity amid the noise.

Again, we all know this world; we've watched it unfold and have experienced its demands in different ways.

So, as we dive into these different scenarios—relationships, career transitions, aging, health, and the impact of living in a digital era - I'm not introducing anything you haven't already encountered. We've all lived through these challenges.

What I'm doing here is putting words to the shared experiences that have shaped us, offering reflections you may find familiar, if not reassuring. It's about recognizing that whether it's dancing through a relationship, facing burnout, or navigating modern life, we're all constantly adjusting, evolving, and learning how to make sense of the complexity's life throws our way.

Scenario 3

David and Sarah - Midlife Crossroads

David and Sarah built their lives together on a foundation of mutual respect, shared goals, and deep affection. In a nutshell, most of the elements we all consider bog standard. A statistically enviable marriage, one that most people aspire to - a seemingly unshakable bond forged over a significant amount of 'quality' shared experiences. Yet, as time passed, David noticed a subtle but unmistakable shift in their relationship, detectable because they were close.

The easy laughter and spontaneous intimacy that once defined their partnership had given way to a routine that felt increasingly mechanical. It wasn't a sudden change but rather a gradual erosion, like a stone worn smooth by the constant drip of water. Conversations became functional, focused on logistics rather than shared aspirations.

They moved through their days in parallel, more like partners in a well-oiled machine than lovers. The lingering thought, "Are we still on the same page?" weighed heavily on David's mind, nagging at him as he longed for the connection they once shared. The solution didn't come in a flash of insight; it unfolded slowly through deliberate re-engagement.

David began to understand that the distance between them wasn't merely about missed anniversaries or forgotten conversations; it stemmed from a deeper emotional disconnect that had grown unnoticed over time. They had fallen into the trap of assuming that love, once established, would sustain itself without conscious effort. Yet, love, like any living thing, requires nurturing and renewal. Instead of confronting Sarah with a list of grievances or suggestions, David adopted a different approach. He initiated small, almost imperceptible shifts aimed at reconnecting on a deeper level.

He began to truly listen when Sarah spoke - not just to the words but to the emotions beneath them. He made a conscious effort to be present: putting down his phone, turning off the television, and engaging with her meaningfully. These changes, though minor, created a ripple effect. Sarah noticed his efforts, and in turn, she responded in kind. The wall of silence that had grown between them started to crack, allowing the warmth of their shared history and love to shine through once more. They rediscovered the pleasure of each other's company, not through grand gestures, but through the simple act of being attentive and present.

As their conversations deepened, David realized that Sarah had been experiencing similar feelings of disconnection. She, too, had wondered if their marriage had lost its spark but had felt uncertain about how to address it.

Their mutual willingness to engage in difficult conversations without blame or defensiveness became the cornerstone of their renewed relationship.

Recognizing the value of having a neutral space to explore their feelings, they sought counselling - not because their marriage was in crisis, but to strengthen their bond.

Counselling provided them with tools to communicate more effectively, express their needs without fear of judgment, and navigate the inevitable challenges of long-term relationships.

Over time, David and Sarah found that their marriage had not only survived this rough patch but had grown stronger.

They understood that a successful relationship evolves, adapts, and requires ongoing care and attention. The key to staying on the same page wasn't merely about holding on; it was about constantly rewriting their story together.

Takeaway

David and Sarah's story reveals that the solution to relationship challenges isn't always about dramatic changes or grand gestures. Sometimes, it's the quiet, consistent effort to reconnect, listen, and engage with intentionality.

Their journey illustrates that love is not a static state but an evolving process that requires ongoing nurturing. By choosing to re-engage thoughtfully and deliberately, they rekindled the spark and deepened their bond.

Nina Simone's *"Feeling Good"* fits because its theme of renewal and emotional freedom mirrors the rejuvenation that David and Sarah experienced as they reconnected and nurtured their relationship, symbolizing a fresh start and newfound joy that emerged from their joint effort.

Artist	Title	Scan QR code
Nina Simone	**Feelin' good**	

Assessments
Take a moment to reflect on your current relationship(s). How do you feel about the level of connection and intimacy? Write down your thoughts.

Identify Disconnections
List specific areas where you feel disconnected from your partner. What changes could you make to bridge those gaps?

Daily Intentions
Set an intention for how you will engage with your partner each day. Whether it's dedicating time to talk or planning a small surprise, write down one actionable step you can take daily.

Communication Check-In
Schedule a time to sit down with your partner and openly discuss your feelings. Use this time to express any concerns, desires, or appreciations without distractions.

Gratitude List
Write down three things you appreciate about your partner. Share these with them and discuss what makes your bond special.

Scenario 4
Complexities – Growth vs Tradition

I've known Emma and Tom for years, and theirs was the kind of relationship that seemed destined for a happy ending.

They met in college, fell in love *quickly*, and built a life together filled with shared dreams, mutual support, and the excitement of a bright future.
They travelled the world, experienced new *adventures*, and envisioned a life as idyllic as their early days together. But as Emma entered her late twenties, a *restlessness* began to stir within her, though from the outside, everything still seemed perfect.

As is often the case when friends embark on their own lives and adventures, Emma, Tom, and I drifted apart.

We stayed in touch sporadically, reconnecting from time to time, but I assumed everything was going well for them. It wasn't until much later that I learned from the grapevine that things hadn't gone as expected.

The song ***You've Changed*** performed by **George Michael** captures this bittersweet transformation *perfectly*, the shift in emotions that Emma found herself facing.

Artist	**Title**	**Scan QR code**
George Michael	**You've changed**	

On the surface, everything appeared picture-perfect. Tom was *kind, supportive*, and deeply in love with Emma. They had a home, plans for the future, and a relationship that seemed enviable from the outside. Yet despite all this, Emma began to feel that something was missing. It wasn't that she didn't love Tom - she did. But the life they had built together, once so full of potential, now felt confining, like a beautifully decorated box that had become too small for her expanding soul.

Emma's restlessness wasn't just a fleeting feeling; it reflected a deeper, existential crisis. She began to question everything: her relationship, her career, her goals, and even her sense of identity. Was she truly living the life she wanted, or was she following a path shaped by others' expectations - society, her family, and even her younger self? This made me reflect on how, in some cultures and religious traditions, people often stick it out through thick and thin for the sake of family, tradition, or religious beliefs, even at the expense of personal happiness. Many are raised with the belief that prioritizing family, duty, and commitment above their own needs is the highest virtue.

People stay in relationships, sometimes for decades, sacrificing their personal desires because family or religious expectations demand it. The idea of pursuing personal fulfilment might seem selfish, even if the heart yearns for something different.

In Confucian philosophy, the principle of filial piety (respect for one's parents and elders) plays a major role in relationships. Confucianism emphasizes the balance between individual desires and the responsibilities one has toward family. This creates tension in modern relationships, particularly when personal goals diverge from societal or family expectations.

Emma's journey is a modern reflection of this dilemma. Like many who face these conflicting pressures, she must navigate the balance between honouring her past and moving toward her future, recognizing that true harmony lies in finding balance within. The emotional weight of these responsibilities and personal desires is echoed in *Tan Dun's Crouching Tiger, Hidden Dragon* soundtrack. The blend of modern and traditional sounds evokes the inner tension between duty and personal freedom, making it a fitting musical pairing for Emma's journey through the complexities of personal and social responsibilities.

Artist	**Title**	**Scan QR code**
Bill Kong, Hsu Li-kong, Ang Lee	**Crouching Tiger Hidden Dragon**	

Much like the protagonist in *Eat Pray Love*, Emma found herself at a crossroads. She realized the life she had once dreamed of was no longer enough. Just as Elizabeth Gilbert embarks on a year-long trip to rediscover herself, Emma knew she had to take bold steps to explore the deeper questions of who she was becoming, despite the weight of societal and familial expectations.

Emma started journaling and reflecting deeply on her thoughts and emotions, confronting the layers of doubt and fear that had quietly accumulated. She also took up new hobbies like painting and yoga, rediscovering parts of herself that had been dormant for years. She began solo traveling, and I noticed a new energy in her when we occasionally caught up. She was breaking free, much like the feeling described in *Feeling Good* by Nina Simone.

As Emma became more attuned to her desires, she realized her relationship with Tom, while beautiful in many ways, no longer served her. The person she was becoming needed freedom, exploration, and space to evolve independently. Staying in the relationship out of comfort or fear of the unknown would have been unfair to both her and Tom.

Eventually, Emma made the heart-wrenching decision to end the relationship, approaching Tom with compassion and honesty. She explained that while she still loved him, her personal growth required her to take a journey alone. Tom, though heartbroken, respected her decision. He came to understand that true love isn't about possession, but about supporting the other's growth and happiness—even if that means letting go. Their breakup wasn't bitter; it was a mutual acknowledgment of the different paths they needed to take.

Even so, the emotional weight of this decision lingered for Emma, much like the haunting mood of ***Careless Whisper* by George**. The song's iconic saxophone melody and lyrics about regret and lost intimacy echoed Emma's feelings of loss and reflection. Although she knew her decision was right, the guilt and melancholy of leaving someone she still loved stayed
with her.

Artist	Title	Scan QR code
George Michael	Careless Whisper	

The line ***"I'm never gonna dance again**, guilty feet have got no rhythm"* mirrored Emma's internal conflict—knowing she had to move forward, but still mourning the past. It's a reminder that even when personal growth is necessary, the emotional aftermath of difficult choices can stay with us, shaping how we reflect on the paths we didn't take. As *Landslide* by Fleetwood Mac (available on Spotify, Apple Music, and YouTube) so poignantly reflects, sometimes change is inevitable, and personal growth requires difficult decisions. The song's reflection on transformation and the passage of time deeply resonated with Emma as she embraced this new chapter.

Artist	Title	Scan QR code
Fleetwood Mac	Landslide	

Takeaway

Emma's journey is a reminder that while some relationships endure out of tradition or familial pressure, others, like hers, may need to end for personal growth.

There's no one-size-fits-all answer, and the decision to prioritize personal happiness over societal expectations is deeply personal.

Emma's story shows that relationships, even when they end, aren't failures – they are opportunities for growth and transformation.

Scenario 5

Jake and Mia - Love in the Digital Age

Jake and Mia, both in their early twenties, met online - a true reflection of fast-food style modern love in our smartphone era. It's a numbers game, nevertheless their connection was instant, sparked by shared interests and long, late-night conversations. It wasn't long before their texting turned into video calls, and their relationship quickly became the centre of their lives. For a while, everything seemed perfect.

But as their relationship deepened, so did the complexities of being connected through technology. The same digital world that had brought them together began to create subtle rifts. Miscommunications through text became more frequent, and social media, which initially was a platform for them to share their happiness, soon became a source of insecurity and comparison. The pressure to present a "perfect" relationship online began to take its toll.

Their experience echoes the themes in ***The Social Dilemma*** **(available on Netflix),** a documentary about the ways social media can distort reality and influence relationships. Like the documentary reveals, Jake and Mia's constant online presence began to impact their emotional connection. The endless connectivity made them feel more distant, even though they were always in touch.

Jake and Mia realized that the digital world was shaping their relationship in ways they hadn't anticipated. They were always connected yet felt less engaged. Their interactions became superficial, reduced to emojis and likes rather than meaningful conversations. Arguments flared up more frequently, often over small misunderstandings born from the lack of real-time, face-to-face communication.

The solution wasn't simply to disconnect from technology altogether. Jake and Mia needed to find a balance between their online presence and their real-world connection. Jake proposed creating "tech-free" moments—times when they would focus solely on each other, without their phones.

At first, it felt strange to be without their devices, but over time, they began to rediscover the joy of being present with each other.

They started going on phone-free dates and doing activities that required their full attention—hiking, cooking, and exploring art galleries.

In these tech-free moments, they reconnected on a deeper level.

"Digital Love" **by Daft Punk** became their anthem.

Artist	Title	Scan QR code
Daft Punk	Digital Love	

A dreamy, futuristic reflection of the tension between digital interactions and real-world emotions. The song spoke to their longing for real connection in a digitally saturated world. They also set boundaries around their social media use. They stopped posting every moment of their relationship online, keeping parts of it private and sacred.

This shift allowed them to focus on building their relationship from within, rather than seeking external validation.

As they made these changes, they noticed an improvement in their relationship. Arguments became less frequent, and their connection grew stronger. They learned that while technology can bring people together, it can also create barriers to true intimacy if it's not managed carefully.

Takeaway: Jake and Mia's story highlights the challenges of navigating relationships in the digital age. While technology can facilitate connection, it can also create distance if it's not balanced with real-world presence.

Their journey shows that it's not about rejecting technology altogether, but about finding ways to be present with one another and build a meaningful connection in

Scenario 6

Evelyn and Henry - Lifetime of Love and Loss

Evelyn and Henry's love story spanned more than fifty years, and it is one I witnessed some of it personally. Built on a foundation of deep affection, mutual respect, and unwavering commitment, theirs was a love that inspired all who knew them. I remember meeting them when I was younger, and even then, you could see it—a bond that had been forged in the fire of life's trials and strengthened through decades of shared experiences.

They met in their twenties and fell in love quickly, embarking on a journey filled with the kinds of moments that define a life—raising children, building a home, and navigating life's myriad challenges side by side.

Their connection was a testament to the enduring nature of love. Yet, in their twilight years, Evelyn and Henry faced their greatest challenge. Henry's health began to decline, slowly and painfully.

The man who had been Evelyn's partner in all things—the pillar of their household—was slipping away. I visited them once during this time, and their once-vibrant home, filled with laughter, had quieted. The sounds of joy had been replaced by the soft beeping of medical machines and Evelyn's whispered words of love and encouragement as she cared for him.

Evelyn, now his primary caregiver, was thrust into a role she had never imagined for herself. She faced the physical and emotional weight of watching the man she loved fade away. I saw it in her eyes when she spoke about him—not just the impending loss of Henry, but the loss of the life they had built together. Despite being surrounded by family and friends, she often grappled with an overwhelming loneliness that came from knowing she was losing him.

In those moments, it was as if the past years of their love played in the background like a song, carrying the weight of time.

"Holding Back the Years" by **Mick Hucknall** often comes to mind - a song that echoes the unspoken grief of watching the passage of time and the yearning to hold onto memories, even as the present fades.

Artist	**Title**	**Scan QR code**
Mick Hucknall	***Holding back the years***	

It encapsulated the silent sorrow of Evelyn's heart, as she longed for the days that were slipping away from her grasp.

But Evelyn's story was not solely about enduring this hardship; it was about her strength, her grace, and the way she chose to approach the final chapter of their lives together. She realized that she couldn't change Henry's condition, but she could change her perspective. She made the conscious decision to focus on what remained rather than what was lost.

In their remaining days together, Evelyn found small moments of connection—holding Henry's hand as he drifted off to sleep, reading to him from his favourite books, and playing the music that had been the soundtrack of their shared life. One such piece, *"Fields of Gold"* by Eva Cassidy, filled their home with memories of golden moments from their past.

Artist	**Title**	**Scan QR code**
Eva Cassidy	***Fields of gold***	

The soft, soulful rendition of this song became a quiet reminder of the fields they had metaphorically walked through together—their life's journey, painted with love, challenges, and moments of beauty.

These acts of love, simple yet profound, sustained her. I poignantly recall her telling me how much those small moments meant to her, how she found joy in them, and how they became a continuation of their love story, even as it drew to a close. In time, Evelyn reached out for support, something she had initially resisted. She joined a caregivers' group and found comfort in the shared experiences of others navigating similar challenges. That group became her lifeline, allowing her to express her fears and frustrations in a space where she felt truly understood.

As Henry's condition worsened, Evelyn had to make the heart-wrenching decision to bring in hospice care. It was one of the most painful choices she had ever made, but it also provided her with a sense of relief. She was no longer just a caregiver—she was able to step back into her role as Henry's wife. Together, in those final days, they shared moments of quiet reflection, expressing gratitude for the life they had lived and the love they had nurtured.

In the end, Evelyn found peace not by avoiding loss but by embracing it. She came to understand that love doesn't end with death; it transforms. The memories they created, the life they built together, would always remain with her. It was Evelyn herself who taught me this, in one of our conversations after Henry's passing. "Love doesn't leave us," she said. "It changes form. It becomes part of who we are."

This story of enduring love, one I had the privilege of witnessing, reflects the profound nature of love and loss. Evelyn's journey showed me—and continues to show all of us—that even amidst life's greatest challenges, love endures, transforms, and sustains us long after our loved ones are gone.

Her strength and grace, in the face of such deep loss, remind us that true love is not just about celebrating the good times but about standing by one another in life's hardest moments.

Relatable music

Evelyn's story suggested the relationship of **Noah and Allie** in *"The Notebook"*, a film that reflects the same enduring love I saw between Evelyn and Henry.

In the movie, Noah cares for Allie as she battles dementia,

never faltering in his devotion, even as she fades away. Like Evelyn, Noah's love remained steadfast, rooted in the many years they had spent together. The love that both couples shared transcended illness, age, and even time itself.

I also feel that one piece of music that Evelyn might have found comfort in is **"Spiegel im Spiegel"** by Arvo Pärt.

Artist	Title	Scan QR code
Arvo Pärt	***Spiegel im Spiegel***	

This minimalist composition mirrors the quiet moments they shared, its delicate notes reflecting the slow, graceful acceptance of love's transformation in the face of loss.

The rise and fall of the music echo the cycles of life and love - moments of clarity and connection amidst the fog of grief.

This musical piece is powerful because it captures the essence of what I witnessed in Evelyn and Henry's story: that love, at its core, is about presence.

It's about the quiet acts of devotion, the courage to face loss, and the understanding that love, even in its transformation, remains the most potent force in our lives.

Scenario 7

The Empty Nest – Departures

After dutifully raising her pride and joy (the kids), Susan found herself in that proverbial boat and feeling somewhat shipwrecked for it.

"What's going on with my life?" as she grappled with the transition from full-time parenting to rediscovering her own identity and pursuing new interests albeit now with a lot **less** physical energy.

Like most people, Susan's home, once filled with the chatter and chaos of raising children, now echoed with silence. She stood in the middle of her quiet home, the emptiness pressing in around her. The once-familiar sounds of laughter and footsteps faded, leaving only silence. She ran her hand along the dining table, remembering years of family dinners that now felt like distant memories. Whilst holding back tears she took a deep breath. 'This isn't an ending,' she told herself, 'It's a new beginning.' For all the bravado, the ache in her heart lingered on.

This profound change marked not an end but a beginning - an invitation to embark on a journey of self-renewal.

The narrative of the empty nest is not just about loss but about rediscovering yourself, painting new dreams, and embracing untrodden paths. Whether its children getting married, going off to university, or even embarking on travels with friends, the empty nest phase introduces a shift in a parent's role and identity. Just like in the

film *Parenthood* (1989), Susan was confronted with the inevitable moment when her children's lives began to expand beyond the family home. In the film, parents face challenges not only in raising their children but in dealing with the emotional shift when their nests begin to empty. *Parenthood* captures the bittersweet nature of watching your children grow, leave, and carve out their own lives, while parents are left to redefine their own.

For Susan, the transition to an empty nest wasn't just about the physical absence of her children but also a questioning of her own identity. Who was she beyond being a mother? *Parenthood* reflects this emotional complexity, where characters grapple with a similar sense of disorientation when their children go off to university, get married, or even venture off on exciting trips with friends. Susan, like the parents in the film, had devoted decades to raising her children and built much of her life around their needs. Now, with their departure for college and marriage, she felt a deep sense of loss but also a newfound opportunity to rediscover herself.

Rather than seeing this period as a void, Susan began to recognize that the quiet held space for something new—a chance to explore her passions, to travel, to reconnect with the hobbies she had long set aside. In *Parenthood*, this same realization emerges: the end of active parenting opens the possibility for a different, more self-focused chapter of life. The parents in the film, like Susan, learn that this transition, though difficult, can also be deeply enriching, filled with opportunities for personal growth.

Each of these narratives—both Susan's and the film's—provides a mirror to our own experiences, urging us to ponder, re-evaluate, and most importantly, grow.

"What's going on with my life?" isn't merely a question; it's an introspective beacon guiding us through life's labyrinth. Like the parents in *Parenthood*, Susan learned that true understanding and fulfilment don't come from external validations but from aligning her journey with her heart's true north. By embracing life's unpredictability and gleaning lessons from every twist and turn, she found the strength to craft a life filled with authenticity, joy, and wisdom.

Takeaway

Life transitions, like an empty nest, offer opportunities for personal growth and self-discovery. Whether its children getting married, going off to university, or traveling with friends, Susan's journey, much like the parents in *Parenthood*, reminds us that it's never too late to explore new passions and aspirations.

Key Insights

Reinvention: Embrace the opportunity for self-discovery and personal growth during life transitions, just as the parents in *Parenthood* learn to adjust to their new roles when their children move on.

Celebrate Independence: Acknowledge and celebrate the achievements and independence of loved ones while focusing on your own journey.

These real-life scenarios illustrate the multifaceted nature of the question, "What's going on with my life?" It's a question that arises in moments of change, self-reflection, and growth. By examining these relatable situations, we gain valuable insights into the complexities of our own journeys and find inspiration to navigate our paths with intention, authenticity, and resilience.

The Unspoken Transition

Our journey through life is replete with milestones, each bringing its unique blend of joys, challenges, and learnings.

One of these significant life markers, especially for parents, is the phenomenon colloquially known as the *Empty Nest Syndrome*.

It's a phase of life marked not by what is present but by an echoing **absence, an empty room, a quiet house.**

In ***Parenthood***, this transition is depicted with nuance, as parents face not only the practical realities of their children growing up, getting married, or going off to university, but the emotional vacuum that follows when the home is no longer bustling with energy.

The term ***Empty Nest Syndrome*** refers to the feelings of melancholy and loneliness that parents or guardians can experience after their children have grown up and left their childhood homes—whether for college, marriage, work, or even a trip around the world with friends.

This transition can evoke a myriad of emotions, from pride in their children's independence to a deep sense of loss.

In ***Parenthood***, we see these emotions play out in various ways as the characters navigate the difficult balance of letting go while maintaining their identity.

Emotional Whirlwind - Loss of Identity

For many parents, especially those who were full-time caregivers, their child's upbringing becomes an integral part of their identity. When that role diminishes, it can lead to an identity crisis of sorts, with questions like "Who am I beyond being a parent?" This theme runs deep in Parenthood, where characters struggle with their evolving roles as parents, partners, and individuals when their children leave to get married or pursue their dreams.

Kylie Minogue's "Spinning Around" mirrors the theme of Loss of Identity in parenthood, capturing the process of rediscovering oneself after change. Just as the song reflects reclaiming confidence, parents may struggle to redefine themselves when their caregiving role diminishes.

Artist	Title	Scan QR code
Kylie Minogue	***Spinning around***	

Sudden Silence

The lively energy children bring - their music, laughter, and even their arguments - becomes a constant part of the backdrop. When that fades, the sudden quiet can be unsettling. However, *Parenthood* reminds us that this challenging phase also holds potential for a reboot. Though it may not feel that way at first, the empty nest period offers opportunities for self-reflection and growth. It can be a chance to rediscover old passions, learn new skills, or embark on fresh adventures, much like the parents in *Parenthood* eventually realize!

Key Insights

Embrace Change

The empty nest phase, like in *Parenthood,* is an opportunity to reflect and reinvent oneself as a parent, partner, and individual.

Reconnect

Use this time to strengthen bonds with partners and explore new interests together, as seen in the characters' journeys in the film, when they reconnect and redefine their relationships in the absence of their children.

Scenario 8

Mark - Fastlane

Mark had always believed that success was defined by numbers - profits, accolades, and the relentless pursuit of bigger deals. He lived life in the fast lane, thriving on the high-stakes adrenaline of his executive position in a cutthroat industry.

His days blurred into one another, a series of rapid-fire meetings, late-night strategy sessions, and caffeine-fuelled negotiations. To him, the rush was everything, the pulse of his life beating in sync with the stock market tickers and the next big win.

What he hadn't accounted for, in his meticulously planned world, was the cost of that rush. He had always assumed he could push his body to its limits, that his drive alone could sustain him. And for a time, it did. But life has a way of interrupting even the most controlled plans with moments that bring everything to a screeching halt. For Mark, that moment arrived without warning - a routine check-up, a doctor's grave expression, and a diagnosis that shook his foundation. The words hung in the air, heavier than any failed deal: "It's imperative you make drastic lifestyle changes, Mark. Your body won't keep up this pace much longer."

Suddenly, the numbers that had once been his lifeline felt trivial. The success that had fuelled his ego now seemed empty, overshadowed by the stark reminder of his mortality. His empire of achievements crumbled under the weight of a simple truth: without health, there is no success.

Artist	Title	Scan QR code
Richard Strauss	Sprach Zarathustra	

It was a wake-up call, one that mirrored the intensity of Richard Strauss's *Also Sprach Zarathustra*, a grand and sweeping composition that symbolized **awakening and transformation**. The thunderous opening of the piece echoed in Mark's mind as he faced this turning point. He had been operating under the illusion that he could power through life, but now, like the protagonist in *2001: A Space Odyssey*, he was on the brink of an evolution—a rebirth, where the metrics of success were no longer external but internal.

His transformation didn't happen overnight. At first, Mark resisted. Old habits die hard, especially when they're ingrained in the fabric of your identity. But the diagnosis was unforgiving, a constant reminder that there was no shortcut out of this. Slowly, he began to make changes. The late nights, once spent poring over contracts, were replaced with the unfamiliar luxury of sleep. Meals, once an afterthought, became a central part of his routine, as he learned the value of nutrition and balance. Exercise, which had been neglected for years, became a non-negotiable part of his schedule. Much like the young entrepreneurs in *The Social Network*, who chased fame and fortune at the expense of everything else, Mark had been consumed by his desire for success. But now, he was beginning to understand the hollowness that comes with neglecting what truly matters. In the film, we watch as the protagonist's empire grows, but so too does the cost—relationships fracture, integrity is compromised, and loneliness sets in. Mark had experienced a similar unravelling.

Artist	Title	Scan QR code
Jesse Eisenberg	**The Social Network**	

He had lost touch with the people who mattered most, disconnected from himself in the pursuit of external validation.

But as he embraced his transformation, the clarity he had once sought in financial gains began to emerge in his personal life. He reconnected with his family, no longer distracted by the constant churn of work. He became more present, more grounded. The success that had once driven him seemed insignificant compared to the sense of peace and fulfilment he found in his new, balanced life.

His colleagues were the first to notice the change. Where once Mark had been the model of corporate aggression, he now radiated a calm confidence. His sharp edges had softened, replaced by a quiet strength. And as his transformation deepened, so too did his influence. People sought him out, not just for business advice, but for guidance on how to achieve the balance that had eluded so many of them.

Mark had become more than just a successful executive—he had become a beacon of possibility, a reminder that true success is not found in the numbers, but in how well we live.

In the end, Mark's story was not just one of survival; it was a story of triumph. Like the soaring notes of *Also Sprach Zarathustra*, his life had reached a crescendo—one that celebrated not just his professional success, but his personal rebirth. He had redefined what it meant to live in the fast lane, proving that true success lies not in the speed of the race, but in knowing when to slow down.

Takeaway

Mark's journey serves as a powerful reminder that true success is not measured by the relentless pursuit of external achievements but by the balance we maintain between ambition and self-care. In a world that glorifies productivity and speed, his story underscores the critical importance of prioritizing health and well-being above all else. Like the grand awakening of *Also Sprach Zarathustra*, Mark's transformation reflects a deeper truth: we cannot afford to sacrifice our health for the illusion of success.

His story is a wake-up call for all of us, illustrating that without health, even the greatest triumphs mean little.

Summaries of Scenarios

These scenarios, while diverse in their experiences, share a common thread: love is an evolving journey that requires continuous reflection, effort, and personal growth. Whether navigating professional challenges, personal evolution, or enduring hardships, love in its various forms challenges us to align with our values and prioritize connection, both with others and ourselves.

*Key **Insights** and **Takeaways** from each **scenario***

Scenario 1

Childhood, where did the seasons go?

Insight: The concept of childhood has transformed over the years. Where once children played outdoors and let imagination guide their days, today's playgrounds are screens, and friendships often form online. This shift reflects a broader societal change, but many parents still encourage their kids to learn instruments, join sports teams, and get involved in creative activities. David and Sarah's story shows that the essence of childhood—joy, creativity, and discovery—can thrive even amidst change, if we nurture it intentionally.

Takeaway: The innocence and creativity of childhood require active protection. By encouraging real-world experiences and meaningful connections, parents can help keep the magic of childhood alive.

Key Action: Create opportunities for your children to engage in hands-on activities, outdoor play, and real social connections. Balance technology use with experiences that cultivate creativity, resilience, and wonder.

Scenario 2

Sarah (The Career Crossroads)

Insight: Sarah's high-powered corporate career, once a source of pride, gradually left her feeling disconnected from her deeper purpose. Like *The Devil Wears Prada*, she questioned whether the sacrifices for success were worth the cost to her happiness. Her journey illustrates the challenge of aligning one's career with personal values, reminding us that true fulfilment comes from within, not from external achievements.

Takeaway: Career success is hollow without personal fulfilment. Aligning your career with your personal values leads to a deeper sense of purpose and satisfaction.

Key Action: Regularly assess whether your career is aligned with your core values. If it isn't, take steps to explore other paths that fulfil both your professional and personal needs.

Scenario 3

David and Sarah (The Midlife Crossroads)

Insight: David and Sarah drifted into a routine, losing the spark in their relationship. Their story shows that love requires ongoing attention and effort to keep the connection alive. By making small but deliberate changes, they reignited their bond and rebuilt their emotional intimacy.

Takeaway: Love needs constant nurturing. Relationships don't sustain themselves; they require conscious, ongoing efforts to remain strong.

Key Action: Make time for daily, intentional connections with your partner. Whether through meaningful conversation or small acts of kindness, consistent efforts can strengthen your relationship.

Scenario 4

Emma and Tom (The Quest for Growth and Tradition)

Insight: Emma found herself growing in a direction that no longer aligned with her relationship with Tom. Like in *Eat Pray Love*, her desire for personal fulfilment required leaving behind the comfort of a stable relationship. Her story highlights the difficult choices we face when personal growth takes precedence overstaying in a relationship that no longer serves us.

Takeaway: Sometimes love means letting go for personal growth. Individual evolution may require stepping away from relationships that no longer fit who we are becoming.

Key Action: Reflect on whether your relationship supports your personal growth. If it doesn't, assess whether staying is a sacrifice that limits your potential.

Scenario 5

Jake and Mia (Navigating Love in the Digital Age)

Insight: Jake and Mia's relationship, strained by social media and external pressures, reflects the challenges of maintaining authenticity in a world that values appearances. Their story reminds us that real connection requires honesty, transparency, and intentionality, even when digital distractions are at play.

Takeaway: In a world dominated by digital interactions, authentic love must be nurtured through real, meaningful connections.

Key Action: Limit digital distractions in your relationship. Prioritize face-to-face interactions and open communication to cultivate trust and depth in your connection.

Scenario 6

Evelyn and Henry

(The Endurance of Love Through Challenges)

Insight: Evelyn and Henry's love remained strong even in the face of illness and other hardships. Their story exemplifies the endurance of love when rooted in commitment and emotional support, showing that love can be a source of strength through life's toughest trials.

Takeaway: Enduring love is built on commitment, trust, and resilience. Love transcends physical challenges when partners provide emotional support and care.

Key Action: Cultivate emotional intimacy with your partner by creating a foundation of trust, empathy, and ongoing care that can sustain your relationship through hard times.

Scenario 7

Empty Nest

While the initial stages might be tough, accepting and celebrating your child's independence—whether they're getting married, heading off to university, or travelling with friends—can be empowering.

It's a testament to successful parenting—nurturing an individual capable of taking on the world. The journey of raising children and then letting them go to carve their paths is a testament to life's intricate dance of holding on and letting go.

The Empty Nest Syndrome, with its challenges and opportunities, is just another chapter in this beautiful, ever-evolving story of life. And like the characters in Parenthood, we learn that this phase, though bittersweet, is filled with moments of growth, joy, and new beginnings.

Scenario 8

Mark (The Health Wake-Up Call)

Insight:
Mark's unrelenting pursuit of career dominance placed his health on the back burner until he encountered a seismic wake-up call—his body rebelled, and his life unravelled. His story illustrates that genuine success is not a singular pursuit of accolades or financial reward, but an intricate dance of well-being, fulfilment, and authentic connection.

Takeaway:
Self-care is the cornerstone of all meaningful relationships, personal or professional. A body neglected becomes a life destabilized. When health fails, the foundation for joy, productivity, and love crumbles. No achievement, however grand, can mask the emptiness left by a body and mind in disrepair.

Key Action:
Mark's revelation serves as a vital reminder to proactively nurture your physical and emotional well-being. Make routine self-assessments, ensuring your ambitions are not unwittingly compromising the richness of your relationships or the depth of your personal happiness.

Chapter 4

"Why Do I Feel Like This?"

Having understood the external challenges we face, it's time to turn inward and understand how these challenges affect our emotional well-being.

We've all been there - caught in a whirlwind of emotions that seem to come out of nowhere, leaving us wondering, "Why do I feel like this?" Emotions can be tricky; they don't always make sense, and they often catch us off guard.

But here's the thing: every emotion, no matter how puzzling or uncomfortable, serves a purpose.

This chapter dives deep into the complex world of emotions, offering practical insights and strategies to help you navigate them with greater understanding and resilience.

Emotions can be as confusing as they are powerful. We've all had moments where we're hit by a wave of feelings that seem to come out of nowhere, leaving us questioning, "Why do I feel like this?" Understanding these emotional states and knowing how to navigate them can be challenging, but it's essential for living a balanced and fulfilling life.

This chapter delves into common emotional scenarios, explores their underlying causes, and provides practical strategies to help you manage them effectively. Additionally, we'll touch on the role of conflict resolution in maintaining emotional well-being, especially in relationships.

Emotions are universal, but the way we experience and express them can be heavily influenced by our cultural backgrounds. For example, in some cultures, expressing emotions like sadness or anger is discouraged, leading individuals to internalize these feelings rather than seeking support. On the other hand, some cultures encourage open emotional expression, which can offer a different path to emotional healing. It's important to recognize how your cultural upbringing may shape your emotional landscape and to find a balance that allows you to process your emotions healthily.

The Weight of Uncertainty

Emily's story is a familiar one - she was constantly plagued by uncertainty about her future. The anxiety of not knowing what was coming next kept her awake at night, questioning every decision she made.

"Why do I feel like this?" she often wondered, feeling overwhelmed by the unpredictability of life. What Emily learned is that uncertainty is a natural part of life. It's uncomfortable, but it's also a sign that you're alive and moving forward. She began to embrace uncertainty by grounding herself in the present moment, practicing mindfulness, and focusing on what she could control rather than what she couldn't. She also learned to be more flexible with her plans, understanding that life rarely follows a straight path.

Takeaway

Uncertainty is a common human experience. Instead of fighting it, try embracing the unknown as a part of your journey. Practice mindfulness, set flexible goals, and remind yourself that it's okay not to have all the answers. These strategies can help you manage the anxiety that often accompanies uncertainty.

Navigating the Maze of Sadness

David had everything he thought he needed for a happy life - yet he often found himself sinking into deep sadness. "**Why can't I shake this off**?" he asked himself, confused by the disconnect between his life's circumstances and his emotional state.

Through therapy, David uncovered that his sadness was tied to unprocessed grief and unmet emotional needs from his past.

He learned that acknowledging and expressing his feelings was the first step toward healing.

David began journaling to explore his emotions, engaged in regular therapy sessions, and reached out to trusted friends to talk about his struggles.

This openness allowed him to confront the root causes of his sadness and begin the process of healing.

As David navigated his emotional maze, a certain piece of music provided a soundtrack to his healing journey - Ramsey Lewis' "Sun Goddess."

Artist	Title	Scan QR code
Ramsay Lewis	The Sun Goddess	

The song's smooth, soulful piano melodies invite reflection, with an underlying warmth that speaks to the possibility of healing and renewal.

Just like David's journey, the song moves from quiet introspection to an uplifting, optimistic rhythm, reminding us that even in our darkest moments, there is light on the horizon.

To accompany your own reflections, listen to "Sun Goddess." Let its soothing notes guide you as you, too, explore the path toward emotional clarity and healing.

Takeaway

Sadness can often stem from unprocessed emotions or unmet needs. It's important to acknowledge these feelings rather than suppress them. Journaling, seeking therapy, and talking to supportive friends can help you explore and address the underlying causes of sadness, leading to emotional healing.

Loneliness in a Crowd

I think back to Sarah, someone I knew long ago, though we've since lost touch. She was always the life of the party—at least on the surface. To those around her, she moved effortlessly from one group to another, her laughter lighting up every room she entered. But beneath that, there was a deeper, quieter Sarah, a side not many saw. I was one of the few she trusted enough to reveal it to.

She would sometimes say, "I don't understand it. I'm surrounded by people, yet I feel more alone than ever." Her words lingered in the air, heavy with frustration. How could someone so intertwined with the lives of others feel so profoundly disconnected? It took time, but slowly, Sarah began to uncover the heart of her loneliness: emotional isolation. She was physically present, yet emotionally absent—an observer in her own life.

For years, Sarah held back, terrified to let anyone truly see her vulnerabilities. It wasn't that she didn't crave deeper connections, but the fear of being truly seen, and perhaps misunderstood, kept her at arm's length. She knew when to laugh, when to speak, but the real Sarah—the one filled with doubt, fear, and longing—remained hidden from view.

After a family gathering, we had one of those rare, unfiltered conversations. "I was surrounded by everyone I love—my mum, my cousins, even my partner—but somehow, I felt like a stranger in my own life. I just don't know how to open up," she admitted, her voice tinged with defeat.

That moment became Sarah's turning point. Slowly, she began the work of dismantling the emotional walls she had built around herself. It wasn't easy. She stumbled, as we all do, and retreated into old habits more times than she cared to admit. But step by step, Sarah started to share her truths—not just the polished updates, but the fears, the insecurities, the dreams she had long buried. And as she opened up, those around her responded in ways she hadn't imagined. Her relationships deepened in ways that no one, least of all Sarah, had expected.

Years later, I learned about a conversation she had with her brother—a disagreement that had simmered unresolved for years. This time, instead of sidestepping it to keep the peace, Sarah chose to confront it. It wasn't easy, but confronting the conflict transformed their relationship. Her brother admitted he, too, had felt distant for years. Together, they forged a new understanding, built on honesty instead of avoidance.

Artist	**Title**	**Scan QR code**
Thank you for hearing me	**Sinéad O'Connor**	

One day, Sarah said something that stayed with me. "It's strange," she began, "but in the middle of that conversation, I remembered a song I'd listened to a long time ago—*Thank You for Hearing Me* by Sinéad O'Connor.

I never really understood the depth of those words until

that moment. It's not just about being heard, it's about being seen—truly understood. That's what I had been missing all this time."

There was a stillness in her eyes that day, a peace I hadn't seen before. It was then I realized how much of our loneliness is bound up in the desire to be known, to have someone hear not just our words, but the unspoken emotions beneath them.

As she spoke, I thought of another song - *Sing* by Pink Martini.

Artist	Title	Scan QR code
Sing	**Pink Martini**	

The lyrics floated to the surface of my mind, a soft reminder of what Sarah had found. "Sing for the laughter, sing for the tear," the refrain echoed. It wasn't just about joy or sorrow, but about the act of expression itself—about releasing the silence we carry within. In Sarah's journey, I saw the beauty of that release, of reclaiming her voice, and letting her true self be heard.

Sarah's story teaches us that loneliness is not merely a matter of being alone. It's about the depth of the connections we allow ourselves to cultivate. She showed me that vulnerability—while terrifying—is the doorway to true understanding. Real connection requires us to brave the discomfort of honesty, to trust that what lies behind our walls is worthy of being seen.

Even in the midst of a crowd, loneliness can persist if we remain closed off. Sarah's journey reveals that it's not the number of people around us that matters, but the openness we bring to our relationships. Building authentic, meaningful bonds begins with the courage to be vulnerable. Sometimes, it's the hardest conversations that pave the way to the deepest connections.

The Unpredictable Nature of Anxiety

Mary's anxiety often struck without warning, leaving her feeling out of control. "Why do I feel like this?" she asked herself, frustrated by the unpredictability of her emotions.

Mary learned that anxiety often has deeper triggers, such as unresolved stress, fear of the future, or past traumatic experiences.

She began practicing mindfulness to stay grounded in the present and sought therapy to explore these underlying triggers.

Additionally, Mary focused on conflict resolution within her relationships, understanding that unresolved tension often contributed to her anxiety.

By addressing these conflicts and setting healthy boundaries, she was able to reduce her overall anxiety levels.

Takeaway
Anxiety can be triggered by unresolved stress or past experiences. Mindfulness, therapy, and effective conflict

resolution can help you identify and manage these triggers, leading to better emotional stability and well-being.

Finding Joy Amidst Life's Challenges

Alex faced numerous life challenges, yet he often found moments of joy and gratitude that left him wondering, "Why do I feel like this?" It seemed strange to experience happiness in difficult times, but Alex realized that these moments of joy were essential to his resilience.

Through his experiences, Alex discovered that joy and gratitude could coexist with life's difficulties. By focusing on the positive aspects of his life, he was able to maintain a sense of hope and optimism, which helped him navigate challenges more effectively. He also learned that resolving conflicts with loved ones, rather than allowing them to linger, created a more supportive environment where joy could flourish.

One piece of music that captures the essence of Alex's journey is **David Sanborn's *"Rain on Christmas."*** This track blends soulful, heartfelt melodies that evoke a sense of warmth and introspection. Sanborn's soothing

saxophone notes convey the subtle, quiet joys that can be found in life's toughest moments, reminding us of the power of resilience and love.

Artist	Title	Scan QR code
David Sanborn	***Rain on Christmas***	

Much like Alex's emotional journey, the song shows how moments of joy can emerge even in adversity—allowing us to find light in the darkest times.

To experience the emotions Alex felt, Scan QR code the QR code below to listen to **"Rain on Christmas"** by David Sanborn. Let its melody guide you as you reflect on finding joy amidst life's challenges.

Takeaway

Joy and gratitude can be powerful tools for resilience, even in the face of adversity. By focusing on what's good in your life and resolving conflicts as they arise, you can cultivate an environment that supports your emotional well-being.

Conflict Resolution - Emotional Well-Being

Conflict is a natural part of any relationship, but how you handle it can significantly impact your emotional state. Unresolved conflicts can lead to feelings of frustration, anxiety, and loneliness, while effective conflict resolution can strengthen your relationships and improve your emotional health.

When conflicts arise, it's important to approach them with empathy and a willingness to listen. Acknowledge the other person's perspective and express your own feelings honestly but respectfully.

Seek common ground and be open to compromise. Remember, the goal of conflict resolution isn't to "win" the argument but to find a solution that strengthens the relationship and fosters emotional connection.

Takeaway

Effective conflict resolution is crucial for maintaining emotional well-being. Approach conflicts with empathy, listen actively, and strive for solutions that strengthen your relationships. By resolving conflicts healthily, you can reduce negative emotions and build stronger, more supportive connections.

Understanding Landscapes of Emotion

Emotions are complex, multifaceted, and sometimes contradictory, but they are also deeply human. The question, "Why do I feel like this?" is an invitation to explore your inner world, understand your emotions more deeply, and use that understanding as a tool for personal growth.

In this chapter, we've explored various emotional states, delved into their psychological underpinnings, and provided practical strategies for managing them. Whether it's uncertainty, sadness, loneliness, anxiety, or joy, each emotion offers valuable insights into your needs and desires.

By embracing these feelings and learning from them, you can navigate life's emotional landscape with greater confidence, resilience, and clarity.

Exploring the Roots

Understanding why we feel the way we do often requires a deeper dive into our past experiences and the unconscious mind. Our emotional responses are not always about the present moment; they are often shaped by unresolved traumas, deeply ingrained beliefs, and learned behaviors from our childhood. Cognitive biases, like catastrophizing or black-and-white thinking, can also amplify emotions, making situations seem worse than they are. By identifying these patterns, we can start to untangle the emotional knots that hold us back and develop healthier ways of processing our feelings

Takeaway

Emotions are not just random occurrences—they're signals that can guide you toward a deeper understanding of yourself and your needs.

By asking the tough question, "Why do I feel like this?" and being open to the answers, you can transform your emotional experiences into opportunities for growth, connection, and resilience. And remember, effective conflict resolution plays a key role in maintaining emotional balance and fostering healthy, supportive relationships.

Conclusion: Our emotions are just one piece of the puzzle; how we interpret and respond to them is equally important, leading us to the next step in our journey.

Chapter 5

"I Know What to Do, or Do I?"

Our ability to address complex dilemmas is often tested, particularly when subtle nuances go unnoticed.

This chapter delves into the overlooked aspects of decision-making, challenging assumptions and broadening perspectives.

Uncertainties often linger in the shadows, even when we convince ourselves we've figured everything out.

You know that feeling – "decision nailed!", only to second-guess everything shortly afterwards - scrolling through Netflix, determined to try something new, but somehow ending up *rewatching the same show you've seen a numerous times* reminding us that certainty is often an illusion. The fallacy of certainty reminds us that we should not fear the cyclical nature of ambiguity and the fluidity of life's decisions. Embracing uncertainty allows us to adapt and grow through in steps. All Actions, no matter how trivial at the outset spurn intended and unintended consequences.

What might seem like a straightforward decision can quickly spiral into a web of results you didn't anticipate. You think you're making a simple choice, but before you know it, you're dealing with ripple effects that were never part of the original plan. It's a bit like reorganizing your closet - what starts off as a quick project somehow turns into a full-scale home makeover. This part of the chapter delves into how even seemingly simple decisions can create complex outcomes and urges us to consider the broader impact of our choices.

And let's not forget about emotions. Whether we admit it or not, our emotional states often have more sway over our decisions than we realize. One moment you're confident, the next you're second-guessing everything because a hint of doubt creeps in. Our emotions can steer us in directions we didn't plan, but they can also be a powerful guide—if we know how to manage them. This section will explore how our feelings influence decision-making and offer strategies for cultivating emotional intelligence so we can make choices with more awareness and balance.

In the end, decision-making isn't about having all the answers or making perfect choices. It's about understanding that life is fluid, consequences are unpredictable, and emotions are part of the process. When we accept that uncertainty is a natural part of the journey, we open ourselves up to growth, flexibility, and sometimes even a little humour along the way.

Art of Adaptability

Life is dynamic, and our initial plans may need adjustment. This section explores the value of adaptability and the wisdom in being open to changing course when circumstances dictate.

There's rarely a single "right" path in life. This part challenges the notion of a linear journey and encourages us to embrace detours and explore diverse avenues.

Sometimes, the best decision is to defer a decision. This section explores the wisdom of patience and the art of strategic procrastination.

Our intuition can offer valuable insights, even when we can't articulate the reasons behind our decisions. This part delves into the subtle wisdom of gut feelings and intuitive nudges.

Values are the compass of our decisions, but they can be multifaceted and evolve over time.

This section examines the intricacies of values-based decision-making. Revaluating our decisions can be a sign of growth and self-awareness.

This part encourages us to have the courage to reassess and adjust our choices when needed.

Through these insights, "**I Know What to Do, or Do I?**" challenges us to see beyond the surface of our decision-making processes, fostering a deeper understanding of the complexities and nuances that shape our choices.
By embracing the subtleties, uncertainties, and evolving nature of decision-making, we can navigate our life's journey with greater wisdom and authenticity.

PART 3: TOUGH QUESTIONS

This section confronts unspoken, pivotal questions - the "elephants in the room" driving us toward sharper self-awareness and insight.

Chapter 6	***Answers that Count*** Here, you'll reflect on essential life questions that redefine your purpose, helping you uncover what truly matters at each stage of your life.
Chapter 7	***Who Are You Listening To?*** We'll explore how the voices around you - from family to society—influence your thinking, and why filtering out the noise is vital for finding your own truth.
Silent Power	***Let Your Work Speak*** Embrace the strength of silent resilience, letting your actions speak louder than words and allow your success to become your quiet testament.

Chapter 6

Answers that count

Life has a way of making us pause at different points, nudging us to ask the tough questions we've been avoiding. Whether you're in your 20s, 40s, or beyond, these moments of introspection are inevitable—and essential. This chapter isn't about making you uncomfortable for the sake of it; it's about helping you get real with yourself so you can live a life that's not just busy but truly meaningful. The questions we'll explore here don't have easy answers, but they do have the power to transform your life at every stage.

What Truly Matters to you?

Let's start with a question that might seem simple but cuts to the core: What really matters to you? In your 20s, this might be about finding your passion, figuring out what drives you, and starting to build a life around it. As you hit your 30s and 40s, you might find yourself questioning whether the career, relationships, or lifestyle you've chosen still align with your values. By the time you reach your 50s and beyond, this question often takes on a deeper meaning—are you spending your time on what truly brings you joy and fulfilment?

At every stage, it's crucial to pause and ask yourself: Am I living according to my own values, or am I just following the script handed to me by society, my family, or even my younger self? It takes courage to admit when you are off course, but doing so is the first step toward realigning your life with what matters most.

Asking tough questions about your life and choices can be influenced by your socio-economic background.

For example, someone from a lower-income background might prioritize financial security over pursuing a passion, while someone from a more privileged background might feel freer to take risks. Gender also plays a role, as societal expectations often dictate different life paths for men and women. Women, for example, may feel pressure to choose between career and family, while men may feel societal pressure to be the primary breadwinner. These factors should be acknowledged as you navigate your journey toward self-discovery.

Artist	Title	Scan QR code
Sweet	**Blockbuster**	

Life often throws us into moments of shocking realisation - those pivotal moments when everything changes in an instant. It's in these moments, much like the sudden explosion of sound in Sweet's *"Blockbuster"*, that we're jolted into a new reality. These revelations don't come with warnings, but they force us to adapt, think quickly, and question what we thought we knew.

What Am I Afraid Of?

Fear is a sneaky thing. It's great at hiding in the shadows, masquerading as practicality or even wisdom. But if you dig a little deeper, you might find that fear is what's been holding you back all along.

Fear of failure, fear of success, fear of judgment - these fears can keep you stuck in a life that's far smaller than the one you're capable of living.

Ask yourself: What scares you the most? And here's the kicker—what would your life look like if you didn't let that fear call the shots? Sure, fear isn't something you can just wish away, but you can decide whether it's going to be the driver or just a passenger on your journey. The choice is yours.

What Impact do I want to leave behind?

We all leave footprints in the lives we touch, but have you ever stopped to think about the kind of impact you're making?

Legacy isn't just about building a business empire or becoming famous. It's about the everyday choices that ripple out into the world, affecting the people around you in ways you might not even realize. So, what kind of legacy do you want to leave?

This isn't about writing a eulogy for yourself- it's about living in a way that aligns with the values you hold dear.

- Are you making a positive difference, no matter how small?
- Are you living in a way that, when all is said and done, you can look back and feel proud?

These questions are not so straight forward, but they're the ones that define the kind of life you're experiencing.

What is your relationship with failure?

Discomfort as a result of any perceived form of failure feels acutely embarrassing, especially if on show publicly - feels like the end of the world.

Any form of failure strengthens our coping mechanism in the long-term – *only if we choose to consolidate quickly.* Accept, Learn and Move on. *Do not dwell on it.*

Dead end, or a detour?
How you deal with it says a lot about your mindset and level of maturity. The secret is in learning how to martial your thoughts at the right time.

If you've been treating it **like a stop sign**, maybe it's time to shift your perspective. Failure doesn't have to be the end of the road; it can be the beginning of something new, something better.

The key is to learn from it, to let it propel you forward instead of holding you back. After all, some of the best success stories start with failure.

What are your deepest desires?

Desires are the whispers of your soul, nudging you toward the life you're meant to live. But in the hustle and bustle of daily life, it's easy to lose track of them, to push them aside in favour of more "practical" pursuits. But those desires don't just go away—they linger, waiting for you to pay attention.

So, what do you really want? Not what you think you should want, but what you truly, deeply desire?

Maybe it's time to stop ignoring those whispers and start listening. Your desires are trying to tell you something important - are you ready to hear it?

What is My Relationship with the Present?

We spend so much time dwelling on the past or worrying about the future that we often forget to live in the present.

But the present is all we really have - it's where life happens, where joy is found, where meaning is created. Are you fully embracing each moment, or are you letting life slip through your fingers while you're busy replaying old memories or planning for a future that hasn't arrived yet?

This isn't about ignoring the past or the future - they both have their place. But if you're not living in the present, you're missing out on the only time that truly matters.

It's time to ask yourself:

Am I here, now? And if not, what can I do to change that?

What Am I Doing to Grow?

Growth isn't a one-time event—it's a lifelong process. But it doesn't happen by accident. It requires effort, intention, and a willingness to step out of your comfort zone. So, what are you doing to grow? Are you seeking out new experiences, challenging your beliefs, and pushing yourself to be better? Or are you stuck in a rut, going through the motions without really moving forward?

Personal growth isn't always easy, but it's essential if you want to live a fulfilling life. So, look at your life and ask yourself: Am I growing, or am I just coasting? And if it's the latter, what can you do to kickstart your personal development?

How Am I Handling Conflict, Especially with Loved Ones?

Conflict is inevitable, especially with the people closest to us. Whether it's a disagreement with a partner, a misunderstanding with a friend, or tension with family, how you handle these situations says a lot about who you are and how you relate to others.

Ask yourself: How do I react when conflict arises? Do I shut down, avoid the issue, or confront it head-on? And more importantly, am I resolving conflicts in a way that strengthens my relationships, or am I letting unresolved issues fester?

Healthy conflict resolution isn't about winning an argument—it's about finding common ground, understanding the other person's perspective, and maintaining the connection even when you disagree. Sometimes, like in *Level 42's "Something About You"*, conflict stems from emotional push-and-pull—when love and tension collide.

Artist	Title	Scan QR code
Level 42	Something about you	

The song reflects the uncertainty that often accompanies conflicts in close relationships. Despite the friction, the lyrics remind us *"there's something about you, baby,"* a signal that deeper connections keep us grounded in relationships, even when tensions arise.

At different stages of life, conflict might look different. In your 20s, it might be about establishing boundaries with friends or navigating romantic relationships. In your 30s and 40s, conflicts often shift to balancing work, family life, or managing the complexities of marriage. By your 50s and beyond, you may find yourself addressing long-standing family dynamics or conflicts with grown children.

No matter your age, learning to handle conflict with grace and empathy is crucial. Like in *"Something About You,"* it's about recognizing that disagreement doesn't have to lead to disconnection. In fact, when handled well, conflict can strengthen your relationships and bring you closer to the people you care about most.

The Power of Tough Questions

These questions aren't just exercises in navel-gazing—they're the keys to living a life that's truly your own. They challenge you to look beyond the surface, to dig deep, and to confront the truths that might be holding you back. But here's the thing—asking tough questions isn't about beating yourself up or finding all the ways you're falling short.

It's about being honest with yourself so that you can make the changes you need to live a life that's authentic, fulfilling, and deeply satisfying. So, don't shy away from these questions. Embrace them, wrestle with them, and let them guide you toward the life you're meant to live. Because the answers you find might just change everything.

Psychology - Decision-Making

Decision-making is more complex than it appears on the surface. Our brains use mental shortcuts, or heuristics, to make quick judgments, but these can lead to errors in judgment. Cognitive dissonance - the discomfort we feel when holding two conflicting beliefs- can cause us to make irrational decisions just to reduce that discomfort. Additionally, decision fatigue, the weariness from making too many decisions, can cloud our judgment. Understanding these psychological factors can help us make more informed choices and recognize when we need to step back and reassess our options."

Role of the unconscious mind

Much of our behaviour is driven by unconscious processes—thoughts and feelings that we may not even be aware of. Défense mechanisms, like denial or projection, can keep us from confronting uncomfortable truths about ourselves. Jungian psychology suggests that our *shadow self*—the parts of ourselves we repress—plays a significant role in shaping our identity and actions.

A piece of music that perfectly reflects this concept of the *shadow self* and the complex layer of our unconscious is **"Angela (Theme from Taxi)" by Bob James.**

Artist	Title	Scan QR code
Bob James	**Angela Theme from Taxi**	

The track's smooth, reflective piano melodies create an atmosphere of introspection, drawing the listener into a state of quiet contemplation.

Its subtle shifts in tone mirror the inner journey of uncovering hidden aspects of ourselves - the thoughts and emotions we often suppress. Just as Jungian psychology encourages us to confront our *shadow self*, the gentle, flowing nature of this composition invites us to explore the deeper, often uncomfortable parts of our psyche.

The understated complexity of the piece aligns with the intricacies of the unconscious mind, as it moves between moments of clarity and tension, much like the process of self-discovery. Bob James' *"Angela"* feels like a musical companion to the journey of understanding our inner world, making it the perfect soundtrack for reflecting on how our *shadow self*-shapes who we are.

To experience this introspective journey, Scan QR code the QR code below to listen to **"Angela" by Bob James.** Let its soothing yet thought-provoking melody guide you as you explore the depths of your unconscious mind and the role of the *shadow self* in your life.

Chapter 7

Who Are You Listening To?

Do You Trust Your Instincts?

In a world filled with a cacophony of voices and influences, it becomes increasingly essential to pause and reflect on the sources we rely on for guidance and whether we have faith in our own inner compass. This chapter explores the dynamics of influence, intuition, and self-trust in the context of our life's journey.

This section examines how external voices, such as family, society, and media, shape our beliefs and choices. It encourages us to evaluate whether these influences align with our authentic selves. Intuition is a silent guide within us. This part explores the concept of intuition, its role in decision-making, and how to cultivate a deeper connection with this innate wisdom.

In a world where external influences can often drown out our inner voice, "Who Are You Listening To? Do You Trust Your Instincts?" reminds us to cultivate self-trust, honor our intuition, and navigate the myriad influences around us with discernment and authenticity. It invites us to embark on a journey of self-discovery, where our inner compass becomes a guiding light on the path to a more genuine and fulfilling life. In the cacophony of external voices and societal expectations, it is imperative to discern who truly influences our choices and whether we have unwavering faith in our own intuition.

The journey of self-trust and intuition is perfectly captured by **Shirley Bassey's** iconic song **"I Am What I Am."**
In this powerful anthem, Bassey declares her commitment to living authentically, without bowing to external

pressures. The lyrics speak to embracing one's true self, standing confidently in that authenticity, and trusting your instincts even when the world demands conformity.

The song's bold, defiant tone resonates with the core message of this chapter: that real empowerment comes from within, and that trusting your instincts is the key to navigating life with discernment and authenticity.

Artist	Title	Scan QR code
Shirley Bassey	I am what I am	

In a world where external influences can often drown out our inner voice, ***"I Am What I Am"*** reminds us that self-trust is not only a choice but a declaration of freedom. Bassey's powerful voice serves as a guiding light for all of us to stay true to who we are, to listen to our instincts, and to honour the unique path we're meant to follow.

Our journey through life necessitates a profound exploration of the sources of guidance and the bedrock of self-trust.

External voices, whether from family, society, or the media, often wield significant power in shaping our beliefs and decisions. Yet, we must scrutinize whether these influences genuinely align with our innermost convictions.

It is only by questioning these external narratives that we can forge a path rooted in authenticity.

Intuition, that subtle and often overlooked inner voice, carries profound wisdom. Cultivating a deep connection with our intuition can be transformative.

It serves as a compass, guiding us towards choices that resonate with our true selves, even when they challenge societal norms.

In a world where the clamor of external influences can drown out our inner wisdom, we must heed the call to cultivate self-trust and embrace intuition.

The conclusions drawn here underscore the significance of navigating life's journey with discernment and authenticity, for it is in honoring our inner compass that we find the path to a genuinely fulfilling existence.

Intuition and Social Conditioning

Intuition is often described as a gut feeling or an inner voice guiding our decisions.

Psychologically, it's the brain's way of processing vast amounts of information quickly, drawing on past experiences and learned patterns.

However, our instincts can be influenced by social conditioning—beliefs and behaviors we've absorbed from those around us.

Understanding the psychology behind intuition can help us distinguish between true gut feelings and conditioned responses.

Cultivating self-awareness allows us to trust our instincts while remaining open to rational analysis.

Trusting our instincts is crucial, but what happens when we misinterpret the signals our inner voice is sending?

When we start doubting ourselves or let external influences override our true instincts, we may find ourselves feeling increasingly isolated—even when surrounded by others.

This disconnection from our inner truth can lead to a profound sense of loneliness.

Let's explore this further by examining the nature of loneliness, its roots, and how we can navigate it in the next chapter.

Silent Power: Let Your Work Speak

People are always watching, silently curious about your next move. As Simon & Garfunkel so hauntingly expressed in *"The Sound of Silence"*, there is power in the quiet moments when no one knows what you're planning.

Artist	Title	Scan QR code
The Sound of Silence	***Simon & Garfunkel***	

The moment you start sharing your plans, though, you're giving away something you can never take back: control over your narrative. When you let others in too soon, their opinions, doubts, and insecurities can start clouding your vision.

Maybe you've experienced it—shared a dream, looking for support, only to be met with scepticism or unsolicited advice. Just like in ***"Ain't No Mountain High Enough"***, there's an understanding that you need resilience and

inner strength to keep pushing forward. But you have to protect that momentum, guarding it closely so it doesn't get derailed by others' doubts.

Artist	Title	Scan QR code
Marvin Gaye & Tammi Terrell	***Ain't No Mountain High Enough***	

That's why you need to move in silence. Not because you're hiding, but because you're protecting your energy.

Your dreams are fragile when they're in their early stages. Like a fire, every time you explain yourself or seek validation, you're letting the heat escape. Over time, that fire dies down, leaving you wondering where the spark went. Let your results speak for themselves, like ***"The Winner Takes It All"* by ABBA**—when you're out there grinding, quietly working toward your goals, nobody has anything to criticize. By the time people notice, you'll be so far ahead that their opinions won't matter.

Artist	Title	Scan QR code
The winner takes it all	***Abba***	

The truth is, not everyone wants to see you win. Even those closest to you might feel threatened by your success because it shines a light on their stagnation. Instead of clapping for you, they'll try to hold you back, consciously or not. The more you share, the more you expose yourself to that negativity. The best defence? Focus on your work.

Keep your head down and let your achievements do the talking. ***"We Are the Champions"***—a declaration that victory comes after relentless focus and hard work.

Artist	Title	Scan QR code
We are the champions	***Queen***	

It's easy to get caught up in explaining your hustle, justifying your dreams. But every time you do that, you're opening the door to judgment, doubt, and unsolicited advice. You'll start questioning yourself, wondering if you're missing something, even when you're not. People think they're helping, but their noise can drown out your conviction. Just like the climactic refrain in *"Ain't No Mountain High Enough,"* you need to keep pushing forward without letting those voices slow you down.

And beware of those who steal. Some won't just doubt you—they'll take your ideas and run with them. They'll borrow from your blueprint, putting themselves in a better position while you're left wondering what happened. By the time you realize it, your momentum is gone, and they've moved forward.

The reality is, not everyone deserves to know your plans. Your dreams don't need an audience while they're still

taking shape. Just like in *"The Winner Takes It All"*, victory is often quiet and hard-won—revealed only once the hard work is done. You wait until the walls are up and the roof is secure before you show anyone. The same applies to your goals. Keep the process close to your chest, and when the time is right, let the finished product speak for itself.

The world is full of people who thrive on opinions, offering advice even when it's not asked for. But the only opinion that matters is yours. Only you know the work it took to get where you are, and only you can see where you're heading.

So why give others the power to steer your journey? Just like in *"The Sound of Silence"*, sometimes the best thing you can do is stay quiet, let the world wonder, and save your words for the victory speech.

The most successful people don't spend time talking about what they're going to do—they just do it. They don't seek approval, because they don't need it. And by the time others see the results, it's too late to interfere.

Your dreams need time to grow, protected from the noise, doubt, and distractions of the outside world. Success isn't built in the spotlight; it's built in the quiet moments of relentless work when nobody is watching. It's about discipline and focus, not applause.

As Queen so perfectly captured in ***"We Are the Champions,"*** your victories come after the world has doubted you, and your triumph will shine through in the end.

So don't let the world in too soon. Stay focused. Move in silence. Protect your energy, and when the time is right, let your success speak for itself. The world will notice, and by then, you'll already be miles ahead.

PART 4: EMBRACING UNKNOWNS

These chapters delve into isolation, digital identity, the challenges of remote work, and the role of religion.

Chapter 8	***Perception of loneliness*** Reflects on the emotional turbulence and growth that come with feelings of isolation, urging readers to explore their inner resilience.
Chapter 9	***Technology - Shaping Identity*** Explores how technology influences our sense of self, questioning the boundaries between the digital and physical realms.
Chapter 10	***Digital Nomad – Remote Working*** Examines the lifestyle and challenges of remote work, offering insights into flexibility, independence, and the redefinition of traditional work environments.
Chapter 11	***Does Religion or Faith Matter?*** Investigates the role of faith and spirituality in navigating life's complexities and finding meaning.

Chapter 8

Perception of Loneliness

Imagine this: you wake up and, before your day even begins, you find yourself scrolling
As we've explored how trust in our instincts affects our sense of self, let's now delve into how mistrust can lead to feelings of loneliness and isolation.

Loneliness is a complex and deeply personal emotion that can affect us all at various points in our lives. It's essential to recognize that loneliness is not solely about physical isolation but also about our perceptions and emotional experiences.

In moments of loneliness, it's easy to feel adrift, uncertain of where to turn. Christopher Cross's *Sailing* beautifully captures the essence of this feeling, offering a metaphor for navigating emotional turbulence.

Artist	Title	Scan QR code
Christopher Cross	***Sailing***	

The song reminds us that, just like a boat finding calm waters, there is peace in surrendering to the journey, trusting that we will eventually find clarity and connection. "Sailing takes me away to where I've always heard it could be," Cross sings, invoking the idea that even in isolation, there is a path to serenity if we allow ourselves to be guided by life's natural rhythms.

Seal's *Crazy* laments the notion that we need to be somewhat detached from reality. Have a listen.

Artist	Title	Scan QR code
Seal	***Crazy***	

"No, we're never gonna survive, unless we get a little crazy," he sings, offering a bold reminder that stepping into our authenticity, no matter how unconventional, is a powerful antidote to the isolation we might feel when trying to conform to the world around us.

Loneliness is a universal feeling, but it can manifest differently across various cultural and socioeconomic contexts. In collectivist cultures, where community and family are prioritized, individuals may feel isolated if they do not conform to social norms. Conversely, in more individualistic societies, the emphasis on self-reliance can lead to a sense of disconnection even in densely populated areas.

Additionally, socioeconomic factors, such as living in an underserved community, can exacerbate feelings of loneliness due to a lack of resources and support networks.

Understanding these diverse experiences can help you find a path to meaningful connection.

Subjectivity

Loneliness is subjective, meaning that it varies from person to person. What one person experiences as deeply lonely, another may find solace in.

It's crucial to acknowledge and respect these differences in perception. As R.E.M. reminds us in **"Everybody Hurts,"** everyone faces moments of isolation and pain, but understanding that these feelings are part of the human experience can provide comfort. The song's message is a reminder that we're never truly alone in our struggles.

Artist	Title	Scan QR code
Everybody Hurts	***R.E.M***	

While social media can offer a sense of connection, it often exacerbates feelings of loneliness by fostering unhealthy comparisons and superficial interactions. Be mindful of how your use of social media influences your perception of loneliness. **Everybody Hurts** suggests that, even when life feels overwhelming, reaching out—whether to a friend, a community, or even to oneself—can make a difference.

Cultivate authentic relationships with people who share your interests, values, and passions. These connections are more likely to alleviate loneliness than superficial or obligatory interactions. And most importantly, practice self-compassion and self-care.

Treat yourself with the same kindness and understanding you would offer to a friend facing loneliness. Just as the song encourages us to hold on, nurturing your mental and emotional well-being is key to weathering moments of isolation.

The Young Generation

Embracing unknowns – confidence and purpose

For young people just starting out in the world, having recently left home or finished their education, loneliness can feel particularly acute. The journey into adulthood, with its unknowns and uncertainties, presents unique challenges to self-worth and confidence. But these moments are also opportunities for growth.

Leaving home, finishing school, and stepping into the world for the first time can be exhilarating yet overwhelming. The unknowns seem endless—careers, relationships, identity—and the pressure to "figure it all out" can be paralyzing. But here's the truth: no one truly has it all figured out, and the most important journey you will take is one of self-discovery.

In *The Pursuit of Happiness* (2006), we watch Chris Gardner, played by Will Smith, face immense uncertainty and adversity as he tries to provide for his son while navigating a challenging career shift.

The film is a powerful reminder that resilience and tenacity are more important than certainty, and that success is born not from having a clear path, but from forging one amidst the unknowns.

Similarly, ***Coldplay's*** "**Fix You**" echoes this sentiment, expressing the emotional upheaval and vulnerability that come with starting anew. The lyrics speak to the power of perseverance, of picking yourself up when things fall apart, and finding strength in the process of growth.

Pointers

It's Okay Not to Know Everything: The greatest myth we're often told is that we need to have a clear path from the start. The reality is that the unknowns are what make your journey unique. Trust that you'll figure things out as you go. This is a time of exploration, not perfection.

Resilience is More Important Than Certainty: Life, particularly at the start of your career or relationships, is full of unexpected twists. What will carry you through is not certainty, but resilience.

Failures Are Not Final: Early in life, we often see failures as devastating, but they are simply steps toward figuring out what works.

Authenticity is Key: As you begin building your career and relationships, focus on being true to who you are rather than moulding yourself to fit the expectations of others.

The Journey Is Your Own: Avoid comparisons and trust that your journey is uniquely yours.

Key Takeaways

- Embrace Uncertainty
- Resilience Over Perfection
- Failures Are Lessons
- Authenticity Matters
- Stay on Your Path

Underlying state

Loneliness is not defined as merely being physically alone; it's deeply connected to our self-perception and social connections.

Attachment theory suggests that our early relationships with caregiver's shape how we connect with others as adults.

Those with insecure attachment styles might feel lonely even in relationships, constantly fearing rejection or intimacy.

Social comparison theory also plays a role, where we measure our worth against others, often leading to feelings of inadequacy and isolation.

By understanding these psychological underpinnings, we can better address the root causes of loneliness and work towards forming healthier, more fulfilling connections.

Men

Power of Experience – appeal of maturity

For many men, particularly as they age, societal expectations can lead to an even deeper sense of isolation, especially when comparing themselves to younger, seemingly more vital versions of themselves. But the reality of self-worth for men lies in understanding the power of experience. Oh, just in case you thought that I might be auditing my own books by writing about Men, there are no get out of jail free cards on offer for Men here.

As men age, they may find themselves facing the inevitable comparisons to younger, seemingly more vigorous versions of themselves. Often, this can lead to a decline in self-confidence, driven by society's obsession with youth and fitness. But here's the truth: the appeal of an older man lies not in competing with the energy of youth, but in embracing the deep wisdom and calm that only come with experience.

In *The Intern* (2015), Robert De Niro's character, Ben, embodies the quiet allure of a man who knows who he is. He doesn't chase approval or validation from others, and his steadfastness and wisdom are what make him magnetic to the people around him.

Similarly, *Fleetwood Mac's* "Landslide" captures the inevitability of change, of growing older and wiser. The song reflects the strength found in embracing life's transformations rather than resisting them.

A few pointers

Confidence Rooted in Experience: Younger men may thrive on impulsivity and boldness, but your strength lies in your ability to remain calm under pressure.

Purpose is Attractive: A clear sense of purpose and direction is one of the most magnetic qualities a man can possess.

Embrace Patience and Thoughtfulness: While younger men may rush into situations impulsively, your ability to reflect and respond thoughtfully is a rare and valuable trait.

Authenticity Over Approval: One of the most attractive qualities in a man is the lack of need to please others.

Emotional Maturity is Key: Women appreciate emotional maturity, honesty, and vulnerability—traits that often take years to cultivate.

Takeaways

- Confidence Rooted in Experience
- Purpose is Attractive
- Embrace Patience
- Authenticity Over Approval
- Emotional Depth

Women

Maturity – Embracing confidence

For women, the journey toward self-acceptance and confidence as they age presents its own unique challenges. With societal pressures often centred around maintaining youthful beauty, many women may feel a sense of diminishing value. But just as with men, this narrative is not only flawed—it overlooks the quiet power and allure of experience.

In ***It's Complicated* (2009),** Meryl Streep's character, Jane, epitomizes this evolution. She is no longer driven by the need to please others or fit into anyone's Mold. Instead, she moves through life with a sense of clarity, authenticity, and humour that captivates everyone around her.

This evolution of self-assuredness and empowerment is beautifully captured in **Chaka Khan's iconic anthem, *"I'm Every Woman."***

Artist	Title	Scan QR code
Chaka Khan	**I'm every Woman**	

This song is a bold declaration of a woman's multifaceted power. It celebrates the fact that women embody endless potential, confidence, and strength at every stage of life. From nurturing loved ones to conquering personal goals, a woman's essence is vast, limitless. This aligns perfectly with the message that women's worth is not defined by external validation but rooted in their inner resilience and authenticity.

Similarly, ***Adele's*** **"Turning Tables"** speaks to a woman's ability to reclaim her power after feeling diminished or undervalued. The song's message of emotional resilience and self-empowerment is a reminder that a woman's worth is not tethered to external validation but rooted in her inner strength.

Confidence is Unmatched:
With age comes the freedom to stop seeking approval from others.

Embrace Your Experience:
Life experience is invaluable, and the wisdom that comes with it makes you uniquely attractive.

Authenticity Over Perfection:
Perfection is an illusion that society often imposes on women.

Emotional Resilience:
Your ability to overcome challenges and grow stronger with each experience is incredibly powerful.

Self-Worth Comes from Within:
As you age, your self-worth becomes untethered from the opinions of others.

Takeaways:
Confidence is Unmatched, Wisdom is attractive,

Authenticity over perfection, Emotional strength**.** *Self-worth from comes from within.*

A song that powerfully encapsulates this journey of moving beyond fear and reclaiming personal strength is **Gloria Gaynor's iconic *I Will Survive.***

Artist	Title	Scan QR code
Gloria Gaynor	I will Survive	

Released in 1978, this anthem of resilience quickly became a universal declaration for those overcoming emotional hardship. This song, with its infectious disco beat and unforgettable lyrics, transcended its time, speaking to anyone finding their strength in the face of adversity. At first, the protagonist is vulnerable and dependent, singing,

"At first I was afraid, I was petrified, kept thinking I could never live without you by my side..."

But through her journey, she discovers her inner power and resilience:

"I grew strong, and I learned how to get along.*"** This powerful message of survival perfectly mirrors the personal transformation we're discussing here. Whether you're moving on from a relationship, breaking free from a limiting environment, or rediscovering your own strength, ***I Will Survive reminds us that not only can we endure adversity, but we can emerge stronger. It's a testament to the idea that true survival is not about merely getting by-it's about thriving

Embracing Solitude

Often, what we perceive as loneliness is an opportunity—a space for reflection and growth. Loneliness can become a catalyst for discovering our true selves if we allow it.

The first step toward that transformation is letting go of the external sources of validation.

Have you ever found yourself clinging to something or someone that no longer serves you?

Perhaps it's a relationship that once brought comfort but now fuels the silence in your heart.

Or maybe it's a job or routine that once felt purposeful but now leaves you feeling unfulfilled.

This is a common experience, and yet many of us stay in these spaces out of fear—the fear of the unknown, of what lies beyond the comfort of the familiar.

But here's the truth: loneliness is not the absence of people, but often the absence of connection to oneself.

This is where transformation begins—letting go of external validation and stepping into self-reliance.

Practical Tips
Solitude - Self-Compassion

Embrace Solitude as a Gift: Begin viewing your alone time not as a burden but as an opportunity for self-reflection. Use this time to reconnect with activities you enjoy—reading, writing, walking, or simply spending quiet moments in thought. These moments are not wasted; they are a chance to deepen your understanding of who you are.

Mindful Journaling: One of the most effective tools for self-reflection is journaling. Set aside a few minutes each day to write down your thoughts, feelings, and experiences. Allow yourself to express your loneliness or any emotions without judgment. Over time, you'll begin to notice patterns in your thinking and discover insights into your inner world.

Practice Self-Compassion: Be kind to yourself during this process. Loneliness can evoke feelings of inadequacy or self-criticism but remind yourself that this is a universal human experience. Speak to yourself as you would to a close friend, with understanding and encouragement. Avoid harsh self-judgment, and instead, celebrate small steps toward healing.

Cultivate a New Hobby: Engage in activities that bring you joy or allow you to explore something new. Hobbies that require focus, like painting, gardening, or learning a musical instrument, can help shift your focus from feelings of loneliness to moments of creativity and mindfulness.

Limit social media: Set boundaries for how much time you spend on social media. The constant comparisons and curated lives of others can intensify feelings of loneliness. Instead, focus on real-world connections or nurturing your relationship with yourself.

Create a Gratitude Practice: Start each day by listing a few things you're grateful for. This can shift your mindset from focusing on what you lack to appreciating what you have, which can foster a sense of contentment and fulfilment.

Seek Professional Support: If loneliness feels overwhelming, consider reaching out to a therapist or counsellor. Sometimes the process of healing requires the guidance of someone trained to help you work through emotional challenges.

Chapter 9

Technology - Shaping Identity

Imagine this: you wake up and, before your day even begins, you find yourself scrolling through social media. Perfectly filtered images of others' lives flash before your eyes—someone enjoying a luxurious vacation, another displaying their meticulously organized home office. It's easy to wonder why your reality doesn't look the same. Behind every post, though, is a complex life—one not as flawless as it may seem.

We all fall into this social media trap, measuring our messy realities against someone else's highlights. The pandemic pushed us deeper into these digital spaces, where our lives, friendships, and even work took on a virtual form. Now, as the world returns to "normal," this digital dependency lingers. We're left wondering: how do we maintain authenticity when our realities are shaped by algorithms? Like ***The Reflex*** by **Duran Duran**, we respond to this digital environment almost instinctively.

Artist	Title	Scan QR code
Duran Duran	The reflex	

The song's catchy chorus - "**The reflex is a lonely child, who's waiting by the park" -** echoes the way we often feel disconnected and isolated, even when surrounded by a flood of online interactions. The reflex to constantly compare and engage becomes ingrained in our daily lives, shaping how we see ourselves and others.

The Influence of social media

Platforms designed to connect us have also become curated stages where we project idealized versions of our lives. The pressure to post, the likes, the comments—they all create a feedback loop that distorts our sense of self. We chase perfection in a world that thrives on imperfection, often losing sight of who we truly are. Like *The Reflex*, we're caught in a cycle of reaction and validation, striving to meet standards set by algorithms, not by our true selves.

Artificial Intelligence's Subtle Hand

Beyond social media, artificial intelligence (AI) is also influencing how we see ourselves. AI now knows our habits, preferences, and desires—sometimes better than we do. It curates the content we consume and suggests choices we didn't even know we wanted. This invisible hand guiding our experiences raises a critical question: are these truly our own decisions, or are we letting technology shape our realities?

The world of AI goes beyond mere convenience. As automation takes on more human tasks, there's a growing fear that it might also take away human jobs. Many worry that AI will outpace their skills, leaving them behind in a rapidly evolving workforce.

The challenge, then, is not just about adapting to technology but about staying ahead of it - developing the skills that make us irreplaceable, such as creativity, emotional intelligence, and critical thinking.

As we speed through the digital age, shaping and reshaping our identities, we often feel like passengers in a high-speed race. Deodato's Night Cruiser captures this frenetic pace, with its rhythm mirroring the swift changes and decisions we make as we move through both real and virtual terrains.

Artist	Title	Scan QR code
Deodato	Night Cruiser	

Technology can bring immense benefits, but only if we use it mindfully. Maintaining authenticity in this digital age requires setting boundaries and reclaiming control over how we let technology shape us.

David Bowie's *"Space Oddity"* captures the feeling of isolation that technology can foster, while *"Rock with You"* by Michael Jackson reminds us of the power of human connection—a connection we must nurture in real life, not just online.

Artist	Title	Scan QR code
David Bowie	Space Oddity	

The film *Ex Machina* highlights the potential dangers of letting artificial intelligence take over our choices.

In the end, we must ask ourselves: are we mastering technology, or is it mastering us?

As we grapple with the existential questions of who we are in a world driven by technology, the haunting melodies of Vangelis' *Blade Runner Blues* resonate deeply.

The track reflects the quiet, dystopian undertones of living in a technologically driven world, where the search for identity becomes a melancholic journey.

Artist	Title	Scan QR code
Vangelis	Blade Runner Blues	

Takeaways

1. **Reclaim your sense of self**—don't let the curated realities of social media define your worth.
2. **Stay ahead of AI's influence** by honing skills that make you irreplaceable, such as creativity and empathy.
3. **Set boundaries with technology** to ensure that it enhances, rather than controls, your life.
4. **Disconnect to reconnect**—log out of the virtual world long enough to nurture real-world relationships and experiences.

Chapter 10

Digital Nomad - Remote working

Picture this: you're sitting in a café in Bali, sipping coffee as your laptop hums. The view of the ocean stretches out before you, and the allure of exploration beckons. This is the digital nomad dream—freedom to work from anywhere, to live without borders. But as beautiful as it sounds, this lifestyle comes with its own challenges.

The Reality of Remote Work:
The rise of remote work and digital nomadism has indeed brought unprecedented flexibility, but balancing productivity with the desire to explore is not easy. You may find yourself in paradise but unable to enjoy it because of looming deadlines. And while working from exotic locations can be inspiring, the reality of poor Wi-Fi connections and time zone differences can quickly dampen the experience. As this digital shift accelerates, it's hard not to reflect on the broader implications of our technology-driven world. **Jamiroquai's *"Virtual Insanity"*** echoes the feeling of being trapped in a fast-paced, tech-heavy environment where the lines between real and virtual lives blur.

Artist	Title	Scan QR code
Jamiroquai	***Virtual insanity***	

The song's lyrics—"Futures made of virtual insanity now always seem to be governed by this love we have for useless twisting, all the new technology"—capture the irony of a world that offers freedom through technology, but at the same time, leaves us spinning in circles, disconnected from authentic experiences.

Post-Pandemic Shifts:
After the pandemic, remote work became the new normal. But now, as life returns to its pre-pandemic pace, many companies are asking employees to return to the office. The flexibility remote work offered is now being met with resistance. Employers argue that in-person collaboration fosters creativity and teamwork, and workers are caught between the convenience of working from home and the demand for physical presence.

For those who continue to work remotely, there's also a growing concern about isolation. The novelty of working from anywhere can fade, leaving behind a sense of loneliness. And while digital nomads often connect with people from around the globe, these relationships can be fleeting, making it difficult to form lasting connections. In this sense, *"Virtual Insanity"* highlights the paradox of living in a connected world that still leaves us feeling alone and disoriented.

Adapting to a Changing Landscape:
Beyond the struggle of balancing work and exploration, there's the fear of automation. The digital nomad lifestyle offers freedom now, but with AI advancing rapidly, many worry that automation will take over, leaving them behind. How can people adapt? The answer lies in upskilling—continuing to learn and evolve in areas where AI cannot replace human intuition, such as leadership, creativity, and problem-solving.

blues

Remote work offers freedom, but it also requires discipline.

The songs ***"Go Your Own Way"*** by Fleetwood Mac and *"Get It On"* by T. Rex capture the spirit of independence and boldness that define the digital nomad lifestyle.

However, as ***"Virtual Insanity"*** reminds us, the future shaped by technology brings its own set of complexities, pushing us to find balance and authenticity in a world that's moving faster than ever.

Artist	Title	Scan QR code
Fleetwood Mac	**Go your own way**	

Artist	Title	Scan QR code
T Rex	**Get it on**	

The film **Nomadland** illustrates both the freedom and the emotional cost of this lifestyle.

To thrive as a digital nomad or remote worker, it's crucial to balance structure with flexibility and remain adaptable to the ever-changing demands of the workforce.

Takeaways:

1. **Adapt to shifting work models**—embrace flexibility but stay prepared for employers demanding more office presence.

2. **Stay relevant in the face of AI** by continually learning and developing skills that emphasize creativity and human intelligence.

3. **Balance freedom with discipline**—remote work requires structure to maintain productivity and prevent burnout.

4. **Combat isolation** by fostering meaningful relationships and finding a sense of community, even when on the move.

Chapter 11

Does Religion or Faith Matter?

Imagine this: you wake up and, before your day even begins, you find yourself scrolling What drives us to seek answers beyond ourselves? Is it the search for comfort, guidance, or something more elusive the need to belong, to find meaning in a world often indifferent to our questions? In a time where belief systems are as varied as the cultures that embrace them, the question of whether religion or faith still matters strikes at the heart of our shared human experience.

Son of a Preacher Man by Dusty Springfield captures this tension perfectly:

Artist	Title	Scan QR code
Dusty Springfield	*Son of a preacher man*	

"The only one who could ever reach me / Was the son of a preacher man."

It's not just about spiritual doctrine or morality—it's about connection. The song reminds us that religion and faith aren't distant abstractions; they reach into our lives through relationships, through the moments when someone else’s conviction touches us, shakes us, or perhaps guides us.

Religion and faith have historically provided answers to life's greatest mysteries, offering both a sense of purpose and a framework for understanding existence.
Across cultures and societies, they create a rich tapestry of spiritual diversity, and no two people's experiences are the same. The question of faith is deeply personal, and this chapter recognizes that there is no universal answer, only individual journeys.

But here's where it gets complicated.

Challenges and Controversies

While faith can serve as a moral compass or a source of solace in times of crisis, it can also be a source of division.

Just as ***Son of a Preacher Man*** shows the allure of faith through personal connection, the history of religious conflict reveals how belief systems can just as easily drive people apart.
When rigid adherence to one’s beliefs stifles empathy or open dialogue, the beautiful diversity of faiths across the world becomes a breeding ground for misunderstanding. Think about Gregory Porter’s *It Could Have Been Me*.

Artist	**Title**	**Scan QR code**
Gregory Porter	**It could have been me**	

The song asks us to reflect on the circumstances of our

lives and the role fate - or perhaps something greater - has played in where we find ourselves. It's a powerful reminder that faith, for many, isn't just a system of belief but a lens through which we interpret the randomness of life's events. It invites gratitude, empathy, and sometimes, humility. The diversity of belief systems, each with its own interpretations, has historically sparked discord. From geopolitical conflicts to personal rifts, the clash of doctrines and religious narratives has often led to division.
Yet, when we engage with different viewpoints with open minds and hearts, we find that, despite our differences, shared human values run deeper than dogma.

A Personal Journey

Ultimately, the question of whether religion or faith matters isn't something that can be answered by doctrine alone - it's something we all must confront personally. This chapter invites you to embark on your own journey, whether it's through the teachings of an organized faith, a secular exploration of values, or a path that blends the two.

Faith, in whatever form it takes, shapes the way we navigate the storms of life. Consider ***Forrest Gump***, when **Lieutenant Dan**, furious and battered by life, climbs the mast during a violent storm and screams, **"You call this a storm?!"**

Movie	Actor	Scan QR code
Forest Gump	**Gary Sinise**	

His defiance toward God is not about rejecting faith but

wrestling with it. He demands answers from forces beyond his control, searching for peace in the chaos.

How many times in your own life have you stood against the storm, demanding answers, only to find that the real turbulence lies within you? Lieutenant Dan's confrontation with God is not about finding easy answers—it's about learning to weather the storm inside himself. The storm passes, not because his questions are resolved, but because he learns to find peace amidst the chaos.

A similar spiritual reckoning is at the heart of ***The Mission*** **(1986)**, where Jesuit priests in colonial South America face a moral and spiritual conflict that tests their faith to its core. **Ennio Morricone's** *Gabriel's Oboe* underscores their inner struggle as they seek to reconcile their beliefs with the violent realities of their mission. Like Lieutenant Dan, they must navigate the space between conviction and survival, faith and doubt.

Perhaps the real question isn't whether faith matters but whether we have the strength to carry it with us, through every challenge and into the quiet calm that follows.

PART 5: GROWTH & TRANSFORMATION

In these chapters, we confront life patterns, dismantle harmful habits, address the loss of control, and delve into fears, self-confidence, and self-esteem.

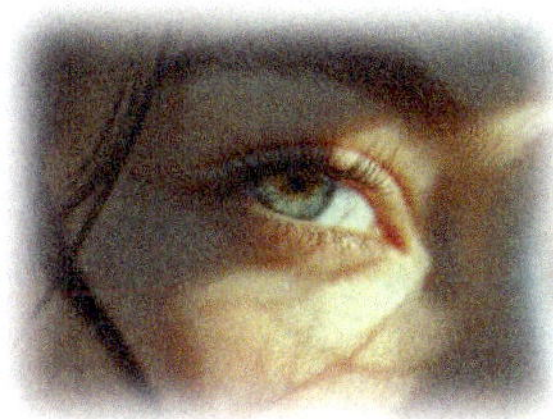

Chapter 12	***Getting Off the Treadmill*** In this chapter, we explore finding meaning in a fast-paced world by embracing a slower approach.
Chapter 13	***Off the Beaten Path – Drink, Drugs, Online Dating*** Here, we confront societal expectations by daring to take unconventional routes and learning from diverse experiences
Chapter 14	***"Why Can't I See Anything Ahead of Me?"*** This chapter addresses the fear of the unknown and explores how to seek clarity during uncertain times.
Chapter 15	***Are You Afraid of Your Life?*** Discover the courage to face self-doubt and confront the parts of life we might prefer to ignore.
Chapter 16	***Do You Trust Yourself?*** We dive into building self-confidence and learning to trust your own judgment and intuition.

Chapter 12

Getting off the Treadmill

Bad Habits

This chapter delves into the intricate web of bad habits and the concept of breaking free from life's relentless treadmill. This chapter provides a comprehensive exploration of the psychology of habits, why we fall into patterns that hinder our progress, and how to escape their grasp.

Habits form the core of our daily lives, shaping our behaviours, routines, and even our identity. While some habits drive us forward, others hold us back, trapping us in cycles of unproductivity and dissatisfaction. Recognizing and addressing these patterns is the first step toward breaking free from them.

Understanding Habits

Habits are automatic behaviours deeply ingrained in our routines. They can either be beneficial or detrimental depending on their impact on our health, relationships, and overall well-being. Acknowledging which habits are limiting your progress is essential to moving forward.

Breaking bad habits is a journey—one that requires both persistence and patience.

Sure, the road's got its bumps, but every small step you take moves you closer to real change.

Overcoming Bad Habits

The process of changing deeply entrenched habits isn't just about altering behaviours—it's about reshaping your mindset.

Persistence fuels this transformation, helping you move forward even when the path seems steep. Patience, on the other hand, reminds you to be kind to yourself, understanding that meaningful change takes time.

It's not about *perfection,* it's about *progress.*

Amy Winehouse's "Rehab" adds a unique depth to this narrative. While the song famously delves into the resistance to change and the complex emotions surrounding rehabilitation, its relevance lies in the raw confrontation of bad habits.

Artist	Title	Scan QR code
Ami Winehouse	Rehab	

Rehab may at first seem a story of defiance, but beneath the surface, it's a reflection of how deeply ingrained habits and personal struggles can be. Amy's candidness in confronting her inner battles resonates with the reality that confronting bad habits is rarely straightforward. The song reminds us that sometimes, the refusal to change is part of the journey, one that ultimately leads to greater self-awareness.

Yet, it's vital to recognize that this voyage, like any journey of significance, will not always be smooth sailing. There will be moments of doubt, periods where old habits claw their way back, attempting to reclaim their dominance. These setbacks or relapses are not indicators of failure but are instead inherent parts of the learning curve. They serve as poignant reminders of our vulnerabilities, pushing us to fortify our resolve and develop strategies to preclude future recurrences.

Central to the success of this transformative journey is an unwavering commitment to the process. Beyond the techniques, tools, and tactics lies the heart's core belief in the possibility of change. This commitment, rooted deeply in our psyche, acts as our anchor, ensuring we remain grounded and focused, especially during tempestuous times.

In essence, confronting and overcoming bad habits is not merely about changing actions; it's about reshaping one's identity, beliefs, and values.

It's a transformation that demands we embrace every facet of the experience - the triumphs, the tribulations, and everything in between.

By acknowledging the importance of staying committed to the journey, regardless of the challenges encountered, we set ourselves on a path toward lasting change, growth, and self-realization.

Forming positive habits

Replacing bad habits with positive ones is a pivotal aspect of long-term success. This section provides guidance on cultivating new, beneficial habits aligned with one's goals and values. Getting off life's treadmill and breaking bad habits can be achieved without the need for a specific list. Instead, you can adopt a more holistic and flexible approach to personal growth and self-improvement. Focus on making one small positive change at a time. Trying to overhaul your entire life at once can be overwhelming and counterproductive.

Start with a single habit or aspect of your routine that you want to improve. Be open to adapting your approach as you go. Life is dynamic, and circumstances change. What works for you now may not work in the future, so be willing to adjust your goals and intentions as needed. Look for sources of inspiration that align with your goals and intentions. This could be through books, podcasts, conversations with people who have made positive changes in their lives, or other forms of media. Surround yourself with a supportive network of friends and family. Share your intentions with them and seek their encouragement and accountability

Chasing Balance in a World That Won't Slow Down

Life, for many of us, can feel like a treadmill.

You're moving - sometimes running - but not necessarily getting anywhere.

You start the week with the best intentions.

Maybe you've signed up for that gym membership, stocked your fridge with healthy food, or even promised yourself to finally get into a solid routine. But as the week unfolds, reality hits. Your job gets demanding, social events fill your calendar, and before you know it, the week becomes a blur of takeout dinners, missed workouts, and an ever-present feeling of falling behind.

It's not that you don't want to prioritize your health or well-being; it's just that life often feels like an endless juggling act. The more you try to squeeze in, the more it feels like you're running in place, just trying to keep up.

The truth is, **we've all been there**. Finding time to stay fit, eat right, and maintain some semblance of balance can feel like an uphill marathon with no clear finish line. But here's the thing: that treadmill can be stepped off. It's not about perfect pacing or following someone else's idea of health; it's about finding your rhythm, stepping away from unhelpful cycles, and moving forward in a way that works for you.

The Fitness Culture Puzzle

Let's start with fitness. Modern fitness culture is everywhere - social media, gym ads, fitness influencers - and it's both inspiring and overwhelming. Whether it's yoga class selfies or intense weightlifting sessions, there's no shortage of motivation out there. Yet for many, this can also feel intimidating, as if you're only succeeding if you're pushing yourself to the limit.

But here's the truth: fitness doesn't have to be an all-or-nothing pursuit. It's not about chasing trends or competing with the person next to you. It's about finding what works for you -whether that's a morning jog, a quiet yoga session, or a few days of strength training each week. The goal is movement that fits your life, not someone else's.

Fitness isn't a race, and perfection isn't the goal. This is where the *Skyfall* soundtrack comes into play.

Artist	Title	Scan QR code
Adele	Skyfall	

Just as the protagonist rises from overwhelming odds, *Skyfall* reminds us that it's not about the fall but how we rise. Adele's haunting vocals and powerful crescendos mirror the resilience needed in fitness—steady progress through moments of doubt.

Your fitness journey, like this song's build, is about pushing through uncertainty and embracing inner strength. Fitness, much like life, is about resilience and adaptation.

And when your journey needs an extra boost of determination, *Eye of the Tiger* delivers.

Artist	Title	Scan QR code
Survivor	***Eye of the tiger***	

Survivor's iconic anthem captures the essence of facing challenges head-on. It's the perfect motivator when you need that surge of energy to power through. Every note tells you to rise up and fight. Whether it's a tough workout or finding the motivation to begin, this song is a call to action -reminding you that strength is earned, not given.

And now, for a touch of fun. As you power through those sessions, why not embrace your inner confidence? Cue *You Sexy Thing* by Hot Chocolate.

Artist	Title	Scan QR code
Hot Chocolate	**You Sexy Thing**	

This infectious groove is an anthem for celebrating progress and feeling good about the work you're putting in. Fitness is more than a routine - it's a chance to feel strong, confident, and yes, a little bit sexy!

Think of fitness like cooking: it doesn't need to be complicated to be effective. A simple, consistent routine can be just as satisfying as a gourmet dish. Just as *Skyfall* reminds us to rise above challenges and *You Sexy Thing* adds a sense of fun, your fitness journey is about progress - celebrating the rise, not the fall.

Life, Work, and Juggling It All

Fitness is just one part of the puzzle, and as much as we might want to prioritize it, life throws plenty of obstacles in our way. For many of us, this begins after university when we enter the world of work. Suddenly, it's not just about showing up at the gym; it's about paying rent, managing bills, and trying to save money while also maintaining some kind of social life. Maybe you're living in a city where rent keeps going up, sharing an apartment with roommates to save money, and struggling to balance long hours at work with everything else. Amidst all that, fitness can feel like just another task on an already overloaded schedule.

And here's where it starts to feel like you're back on that treadmill—moving but not really getting anywhere. When life becomes about just trying to keep your head above water, staying healthy can seem like one more thing to check off a never-ending list. But remember, it's not failure to feel like you're stretched thin. That's reality. You're not alone in feeling that way, and acknowledging the pressures of modern life is the first step in finding a way to deal with them.

Fitness and Relationships
Walking the Same Path?

Let's talk about relationships. Fitness, like most things, doesn't happen in a bubble. If you're in a relationship, you've probably noticed how your fitness habits—or lack thereof - impact your partner.

Maybe you both push each other to get to the gym or go for that morning run, and maybe sometimes it feels like fitness is a way to bond. But what if one of you is all-in, and the other just wants to relax?

Finding balance in relationships can be tricky. On the one hand, fitness can be a great way to connect and support each other. You can go to the gym together, encourage one another on tough days, and share in each other's progress.

On the other hand, it's important to make sure it doesn't become a point of pressure or frustration. Sometimes, one of you might want to take a break, and that's okay. Fitness, like everything else in life, works best when it's built on mutual respect and balance.

Not every workout has to be a shared activity - sometimes, it's about understanding and supporting each other's individual needs.

Temptation and the Busy Life Trap

We all know how easy it is to get pulled off track. By the end of the week, you're tired, the fridge is empty, and fast food is calling your name. The pace of modern life makes it incredibly tempting to grab quick fixes—whether that's takeout or skipping a workout for a night of Netflix. After a long day of work, the last thing you want to think about is another responsibility, even if that responsibility is your health.

But here's the thing: you don't have to be perfect. Not every week will be filled with kale smoothies and daily workouts. Some weeks, you'll grab a burger on the way home, and some days, you'll skip the gym in favour of an evening on the couch. The key isn't in avoiding temptation completely but in knowing that it's okay to fall off track sometimes. What matters is that you find a rhythm that works for you and get back to it when you're ready.

The Power of Stepping Off the Treadmill

Sometimes, the best thing you can do for your health both physical and mental is step off life's treadmill altogether.

We live in a culture that glorifies the hustle, where being busy is often seen as a sign of success. But there's immense value in slowing down and taking breaks.

A holiday or even just a weekend away can reset your mind and body. It gives you the chance to step away from the daily grind, gain perspective, and come back refreshed. Think of it as hitting the pause button. Taking time to rest isn't just about physical recovery—it's about mental clarity. When you step off the treadmill and give yourself room to breathe, you come back with a clearer head and a better

sense of direction.
Sometimes, the only way to move forward is to first stop running in circles.

Breaking Habits: Understanding the Habit Loop

We've all got habits that keep us on that treadmill—whether it's emotional eating, skipping workouts, or simply falling into routines that don't serve us. The key to breaking bad habits isn't just about willpower; it's about understanding how habits form in the first place.

The **Habit Loop** - cue, routine, reward -explains why we fall into certain behaviours. For example, stress (cue) might lead to overeating (routine) because it brings temporary comfort (reward). But the brain's ability to change, known as **neuroplasticity**, means we can rewire these patterns. By identifying the triggers and replacing unhealthy routines with positive ones, you can create lasting change.

It's about small steps.

Maybe instead of emotional eating when stressed, you take a walk or practice deep breathing.

Over time, these small changes can add up, helping you step off the treadmill of bad habits and into a healthier, more balanced routine.

Finding Strength Beyond Weights

While fitness is often seen as a physical pursuit, it's also deeply mental. For women especially, fitness can sometimes feel like it's tied to external expectations—how you should look, how you should act. But fitness isn't about fitting into anyone's mould; it's about finding your own strength. Whether it's through weightlifting, yoga, or simply taking time for yourself, fitness can be a way to empower yourself both physically and mentally. It's not just about lifting weights—it's about lifting yourself up, feeling strong, and knowing that you have the power to shape your own path.

Empowering Music for Women

Music can be a powerful motivator, especially when you're pushing through tough moments. While *Eye of the Tiger* is a classic for anyone who needs that extra push, Beyoncé's *"Run the World (Girls)"* is an anthem for women everywhere. It's about strength, resilience, and knowing that you have the power to overcome any challenge. Whether in the gym, at work, or in life, it's a reminder that you're capable of anything.

Takeaways:

1. **Find What Works for You**: Fitness isn't one-size-fits-all. Find the form of movement that fits into your life, whether that's yoga, walking, or lifting weights. Consistency matters more than perfection.

2. **Embrace Balance**: Life gets busy, and that's okay. It's about finding balance, not striving for perfection. Some days you'll nail your goals, and some days you'll fall short. Just keep moving forward.

3. **Support Each Other**: Whether it's a partner or a friend, fitness can be a great way to connect. But don't let it become a source of pressure. Balance is key in relationships, just as it is in fitness.

4. **Take Breaks**: Stepping off the treadmill is important. Take holidays, breaks, and moments to pause. It will give you clarity, perspective, and the energy to keep going.

5. **Break the Habit Loop**: Identify the cues that trigger bad habits and replace them with healthier routines. Over time, you can rewire your brain for lasting change.

Film: *Rocky* (1976)

Rocky's journey isn't just about boxing - it's about **perseverance, discipline**, and finding the strength to keep going, even when you don't think you can. It's a powerful metaphor for pushing through challenges in life, whether they're physical or mental.

Final Thought

Staying fit and balanced in today's world isn't easy. But it's not about perfection - it's about finding your rhythm, stepping off the treadmill when you need to, and giving yourself the grace to keep going. Take it one day at a time and remember that the journey—though long - is always worth it.

Chapter 13

Off the Beaten Path
Drink, Drugs, Online Dating

We've all heard the phrase "living on the treadmill of life," where you're running but not really getting anywhere. But there's another kind of treadmill—one filled with social expectations, nightlife, dating apps, and the pressure to keep up with the fast pace of modern life. It's a treadmill where, especially within the LGBTQ+ community, the pressures to fit in can feel overwhelming. But just like any other treadmill, you have the power to step off, to find your own pace, and to navigate life in a way that's true to you.

A Spirited Community: The Liberal and Generous Soul of Gay Culture

The LGBTQ+ community, and especially gay people, have always embraced life with a spirit that's both liberal and generous. It's a culture that celebrates diversity, freedom, and the right to live authentically. In doing so, gay people have become cultural pioneers, contributing immeasurably to the arts, politics, and the fight for social justice. They've shown us that to live freely is to live fully.

The beauty of this community is its embrace of difference. Just as no two people are the same, no two paths are identical. In the gay community, there's no single way to express love, identity, or connection. Whether through creative expression, activism, or simply being a supportive friend, gay people continuously offer the world something invaluable—a reminder that living true to yourself is a form of generosity in itself.

The Challenge of Social Spaces: Drink and Drugs

Bars and clubs have historically been places of refuge for the gay community—spaces where individuals can be themselves, connect with others, and feel free from societal judgment. These social spaces are vibrant and full of life, but they also come with their own set of pressures. Drinking and partying often go hand in hand with the nightlife scene, and it can be easy to get swept up in it.

Much like a treadmill, there's a rhythm to it—a sense that you're moving with the crowd, keeping pace with expectations. But as with any form of escapism, there's a fine line between fun and excess. The social scene can feel like a cycle of validation, where the more you drink or indulge, the more you feel like you belong.

But real belonging isn't found in the bottom of a glass. It's found in the moments of genuine connection, where you're seen for who you are—without the mask of substances. Just like with breaking bad habits, stepping off this treadmill requires recognizing your own boundaries, finding balance, and understanding that you don't need to conform to fit in.

A Fantastic Woman: A Story of Strength, Resilience, and Music

One film that brilliantly encapsulates the struggle for authenticity within the LGBTQ+ community is *A Fantastic Woman*(2017). This Chilean film tells the story of Marina, a transgender woman who faces prejudice, grief, and identity challenges after the death of her partner. Marina's journey is both a fight for recognition and a testament to the strength that comes from living authentically, despite societal pressures.

Artist	Title	Scan QR code
Fantastic Woman	Queen	

The film's soundtrack, much like Marina's character, is both haunting and beautiful - a perfect blend of classical and contemporary pieces that mirror her emotional highs and lows. The music underscores the struggles that many LGBTQ+ individuals face in a world that's often unkind to difference.

A Fantastic Woman reminds us that resilience isn't about pretending everything's okay; it's about-facing life's challenges head-on and finding strength in your identity

Relatable Music

There are times when indulgence and escape seem to take hold, as in *Summer Madness*, where the heat of the moment clouds judgment and leads us into uncharted waters. Yet, within that haze, clarity can eventually emerge, guiding us back to ourselves.

Artist	Title	Scan QR code
Kool and the Gang	Summer Madness	

Donna Summer's *Love to Love You Baby* encapsulates the hedonistic, sensuous allure of living in the moment, even when the consequences are uncertain.

Artist	Title	Scan QR code
Donna Summer	Love to Love You Baby	

The Freedom of Legal Acceptance

We're living in a time where, finally, gay people can live more freely than ever before. Thanks to legal protections and societal shifts, individuals are now able to love openly, contribute fully, and live authentically. But this hasn't always been the case. Just a few decades ago, being openly gay came with enormous risks—risks of violence, discrimination, and isolation.

Today's gay community is both a reflection of this hard-earned progress and a beacon of hope for what's possible when society embraces diversity.
The relief that comes with legal recognition cannot be understated - it's a freedom that allows for deeper contributions, greater visibility, and a more vibrant cultural landscape. But even with this progress, the fight for full equality continues, reminding us that authenticity is a powerful, ongoing journey.

The Danish Girl: The Courage to Transform

In a similar vein, *The Danish Girl* (2015) tells the story of Lili Elbe, one of the first known recipients of gender-affirming surgery. This film, starring Eddie Redmayne, is a poignant exploration of identity, love, and the courage it takes to live fully as oneself. Lili's transition, much like Marina's in *A Fantastic Woman*, serves as a powerful reminder that transformation is both a personal and societal journey.

Both films highlight the resilience of the human spirit in the face of adversity and the beauty that comes from embracing one's true identity, no matter how difficult the road may be.

Navigating Online Dating: Connection or Chaos?

In the modern age, online dating has become the new frontier of connection. For many gay people, especially those in areas without a strong local community, apps like Grindr and Tinder provide a lifeline to others who share their experiences. But much like the treadmill of nightlife, these apps can sometimes become exhausting. The constant swiping, ghosting, and fleeting conversations can leave you feeling more disconnected than when you started.

The challenge with online dating is to find balance—between engaging with the world and not getting lost in it. It's easy to fall into the trap of seeking validation through matches, but true connection goes deeper than an app can offer. It's about authenticity, patience, and knowing when to step away to protect your well-being.

Takeaways

1. **Celebrate Diversity and Authenticity**: Gay culture thrives on diversity and self-expression. Embrace the liberal spirit that allows you to be unapologetically yourself.

2. **Balance in Social Spaces**: Recognize when social drinking and partying become too much. Know your boundaries and step off the treadmill when it no longer serves you.

3. **Legal Acceptance**: Appreciate the hard-won freedom of legal recognition but remain aware that the journey toward full equality is ongoing.

4. **Meaningful Connections**: Whether in nightlife or online dating, seek genuine connections. True belonging comes from being seen and valued for who you truly are.

Film: *A Fantastic Woman* (2017)

A powerful portrayal of a transgender woman's journey through loss, love, and societal rejection, *A Fantastic Woman* speaks to the resilience of the LGBTQ+ community. Its soundtrack is a hauntingly beautiful accompaniment to Marina's quest for dignity and self-acceptance.

Music: Soundtrack of *A Fantastic Woman*

With its mix of classical and contemporary music, the soundtrack of *A Fantastic Woman* mirrors the complexities of living authentically in a world that often rejects difference. It's a reminder that the struggle for identity is accompanied by moments of profound beauty.

Final Thoughts

This chapter celebrates the ***incredible contributions*** of gay people to society—their creativity, generosity, and courage to live authentically.

Whether navigating the complexities of social spaces, online dating, or societal expectations, the journey toward authenticity is a powerful one.

As we celebrate the progress made, we must also remember that there is more work to be done - and that the liberal, generous spirit of the LGBTQ+ community is an ***essential part of our shared humanity.***

Relatable Music

There are moments when the night calls us to escape into its energy and possibilities. *Give Me the Night* captures the allure of nightlife, where indulgence and self-expression intertwine, revealing both the highs and pitfalls of venturing off the beaten path.

Artist	Title	Scan QR code
George Benson	**Give Me the Night**	

Sometimes, relationships become toxic, leading us down a path of emotional entanglement.

Tainted Love encapsulates the feeling of being caught in a cycle of desire and rejection, making it a fitting soundtrack for chapters that explore the darker sides of love and self-discovery.

Artist	Title	Scan QR code
Soft Cell	**Tainted Love**	

Chapter 14

"Why Can't I See Anything Ahead of Me?"

The future can feel impossibly murky—like trying to read tea leaves, but all you're getting is the suggestion that you probably need more sleep and fewer existential crises. In these moments, when uncertainty blankets the path ahead, it's as if we're standing at the edge of the unknown, unable to make out what lies beyond. This is a universal experience—a shared sense of vulnerability we all encounter as we navigate life's twists and turns.

The Desire for Certainty

It's only natural to crave clarity, to want a clear roadmap or some control over what's coming. Yet life, in its unpredictable way, constantly reminds us that certainty is fleeting. When the road ahead becomes foggy, it's easy to feel anxious or frustrated, questioning why the way forward isn't more defined.

Embracing Ambiguity

But what if we could see these moments of ambiguity differently? Instead of resisting uncertainty, what if we embraced it as an essential part of being human? Like a mist rolling in, uncertainty brings its own beauty—a beauty rooted in possibility and discovery. Often, when everything seems unclear, we're standing on the edge of something new, something transformative.

The Process of Discovery

Not being able to see the future isn't necessarily a curse. It's in these moments of uncertainty that we plant the seeds of personal growth and self-discovery. The lack of a clear destination allows us to focus on the journey, teaching us resilience, adaptability, and helping us grow into our most authentic selves.

Finding Comfort in along the way

Navigating through uncertainty calls for a shift in focus—finding peace not in knowing the future, but in savouring the present. The unknown becomes less daunting when we recognize that the journey itself, with all its surprises, is where life's richest moments truly unfold.

Samantha's Realization

Samantha sat alone in her favourite park, a place where she often retreated when life's challenges seemed insurmountable. The gentle rustling of leaves and the distant sounds of children playing provided a soothing backdrop to her thoughts. With each passing day, the weight of uncertainty seemed to grow heavier, and she couldn't help but wonder, "Why can't I see anything ahead of me?"

Life had always been a journey filled with twists and turns, but lately, it felt like she was navigating through a dense fog, unable to discern the path ahead. The road, once so clear and well-defined, had become shrouded in ambiguity. Samantha had heard countless times that life was a journey, not a destination, but in this moment, she found it hard to embrace that wisdom.

In her moments of self-doubt, Samantha had often sought solace in the stories of others who had faced similar struggles. She recalled a conversation with her grandmother, who had weathered the storms of life with grace and resilience. Her grandmother's words echoed in her mind: "Life is like sailing on a vast ocean. Sometimes, the seas are calm, and you can chart your course with precision. Other times, you encounter storms that obscure your vision. But remember, it's during those storms that you discover your true strength."

Samantha realized that it was precisely in times of uncertainty that her character was tested, and her resilience honed. Instead of desperately trying to force a clear path forward, she needed to embrace the fog and trust that it would eventually lift. She understood that the journey of life was about learning to navigate through both the clear skies and the storms, finding purpose during the midst of uncertainty.

Relatable Film "Wild" (2014)

Samantha’s experience of navigating through life's fog of uncertainty is a powerful reflection of the human condition. A similar journey is explored in the film **"Wild"**, based on the memoir by Cheryl Strayed and starring Reese Witherspoon. Much like Samantha, Cheryl embarks on a physically and emotionally demanding solo trek along the Pacific Crest Trail to heal from personal loss and a broken past. As Cheryl walks through the wilderness, she confronts the emotional baggage that weighs her down, ultimately learning to detach from the pain of the past.

The film mirrors the themes of uncertainty, resilience, and emotional detachment. Just as Samantha grapples with the fog of her own life, Cheryl learns that the path forward isn’t always clear, but the process of moving through that fog brings growth, healing, and personal clarity. **"Wild"** reminds us that sometimes, it's in the struggle with our past and the unknown that we discover our greatest strength.

Relatable Music

Ralph Vaughan Williams' "The Lark Ascending"

As Samantha reflected on her journey, she felt a sense of calm wash over her—a sense that maybe, just maybe, the uncertainty was not something to fear, but something to embrace. This realization is echoed in the beautiful piece of music **"The Lark Ascending"** by Ralph Vaughan Williams.

Artist	Title	Scan QR code
Vaughan Williams	The Lark Ascending	

The ethereal violin solo, representing a lark ascending into the sky, captures the essence of rising above the challenges and uncertainties that weigh us down. The music begins gently, much like the early stages of self-discovery, and as it progresses, it becomes a reflection of the emotional freedom that comes with letting go of control and trusting the journey ahead.

Much like Samantha's journey through the fog, **"The Lark Ascending"** invites listeners to soar above life's challenges, finding peace and grace in the unknown.

It's a piece that perfectly encapsulates the beauty and power of rising above emotional entanglements and uncertainty, much like Samantha's realization that clarity would come in its own time.

The Art of Emotional Detachment

As Samantha reflected on her journey through the fog of uncertainty, she realized that part of moving forward was learning to emotionally detach from situations and people that no longer served her growth. Emotionally detaching doesn't mean cutting someone out of your life entirely - it's about protecting your well-being, setting healthy boundaries, and creating space for personal clarity.

The first step in emotional detachment is recognizing when it's necessary. Often, emotions cloud our judgment. We stay loyal to people who drain our energy or remain entangled in situations that no longer support our best selves. If you consistently feel anxious or weighed down after interacting with someone, that's a red flag. It's time to listen to that inner voice telling you to create distance.

The second step is to set clear boundaries. This involves communicating your needs without guilt or fear. You might need to say "no" to certain requests or limit the amount of time you spend with someone. Boundaries aren't about punishing others; they're about honouring your emotional peace. Learning to be assertive in protecting your own energy is a form of self-love.

The third step is to focus on your own growth. When we're emotionally entangled with others, it's easy to lose sight of our own needs and aspirations. We may neglect self-care or set aside our dreams in favour of supporting someone else. But the truth is, you can't pour from an empty cup. Prioritizing your happiness is essential for maintaining emotional health.

The fourth step is to release control. Sometimes, we feel responsible for others' happiness or success, believing we can fix their problems. But the reality is, everyone must take responsibility for their own choices. Trying to control someone else's journey will only lead to frustration and resentment.

Finally, give yourself permission to move on. Emotional detachment doesn't always mean severing ties—it could simply mean spending less time with someone or letting go of the emotional weight the relationship once carried. It's about creating a new dynamic that allows you to thrive.

As Samantha sat in the park, contemplating these realizations, she made a promise to herself. She would no longer fret about what she couldn't control. Instead, she would focus on the small steps she could take each day to protect her energy and move forward with clarity. She would create boundaries, pursue her passions, and surround herself with people who uplifted her.

In doing so, Samantha understood that emotional detachment wasn't about loss—it was about gaining a deeper sense of self. It was about creating the space she needed for something new, something better, to enter her life.

Cultivating Resilience

Uncertainty can be a demanding teacher, but it's one that forges resilience. It teaches us to bend with the winds of change rather than break, to adapt to the shifting terrain, and to find strength in our ability to endure.

By embracing the present, emotionally detaching from what no longer serves us, and moving forward despite the fog, we cultivate the resilience to navigate the unknown with grace. Samantha's newfound perspective was not one of fear but of possibility, trusting that clarity would come in its own time. As she rose from the park bench and began her walk home, Samantha knew that the fog hadn't lifted yet. But now, she walked with confidence, trusting the journey and embracing the unknown, knowing that the best was still to come.

Conclusion

This chapter reminds us that uncertainty is a natural part of the human experience and that it's during these times that we often discover our true strength. By learning to emotionally detach from draining situations and focusing on the present, we can find peace and purpose, even when the future remains unclear. Much like the soaring lark in Ralph Vaughan Williams' **"The Lark Ascending"** or the transformative journey in **"Wild"**, embracing uncertainty and detaching from what no longer serves us, opens up a world of possibilities. The fog of life may obscure the path ahead, but it often conceals the most breathtaking landscapes waiting to be explored.

Chapter 15

Are You Afraid of Your Life?

In the quiet corners of our hearts, hidden beneath the layers of daily routines and responsibilities, lies a question we often avoid: *Are you afraid of your life?*

This rare question can stir uncomfortable emotions, one we might prefer to sidestep, yet it holds the key to understanding a key part of our survival toolkit. In the song ***Don't Fear the Reaper***, Blue Öyster Cult encourages us to embrace life's inevitabilities and let go of fear by challenging unknowns as necessary steps towards real progress.

Artist	Title	Scan QR code
Blue Oyster Cult	(Don't Fear) the Reaper	

We all know that fear can manifest itself in so many ways – for example - unknowns, rejection, or even success. It's as if we're standing on the threshold of our own potential, peering into the abyss of uncertainty, and hesitation seizes us.

Let's be clear, the fear of one's life is not a sign of weakness; rather, it's a testament to the complexity of our life. We grapple with the desire for security like paying off the mortgage, educating our children whilst yearning for personal growth through adventure and self-discovery. It's a delicate balance, and at times, it can feel as though we're walking a tightrope, swaying between fear and courage.

In Buddhist teachings, fear is viewed through the lens of **impermanence**, or anicca. Everything in life, including fear, is transient. By learning to let go of attachment to outcomes, as Buddhism teaches, we can begin to observe fear without judgment. Fear becomes not something to be conquered, but something to accept and release. It flows through us like waves, temporary and ever-changing. This practice of mindfulness allows us to face life's challenges with clarity and peace, rather than being overwhelmed by fear.

Music Pairing Suggestion: As you reflect on fear and non-attachment, consider the meditative quality of **Philip Glass – "Metamorphosis Two"**, a minimalist composition that mirrors the stillness of the mind when it lets go of fear and attachment.

Available on Spotify, Apple Music, and YouTube

Film Reference: *The Truman Show* (1998)

Much like the character Truman in *The Truman Show*, we often live within the confines of a carefully constructed world, unaware of the vast potential that lies beyond. In the film, Truman's life is a fabricated illusion, and he is driven by the fear of the unknown. His fear manifests in his reluctance to leave the only life he has known, a life of safety and predictability. However, his eventual decision to confront his fears and step into the unknown represents the courage to take control of one's destiny, a theme that resonates deeply with this chapter.

The film's climax, when Truman decides to walk through the door into the real world, despite the overwhelming uncertainty and fear of what lies beyond, mirrors our own journeys when we choose to confront our fears. By stepping out of the familiar and into the unknown, we embrace our authentic selves.

The Truman Show is available on Netflix, Amazon Prime, and Apple TV+. Its relevance to this chapter lies in its exploration of fear, control, and the courage to face life's uncertainties.

But what if, instead of succumbing to our fears, we chose to confront them head-on? What if we acknowledged that fear is not an obstacle but a companion on our journey, urging us to pay attention, to be alert, to be fully alive?

In those moments when fear threatens to paralyze us, it's worth remembering that some of life's most profound experiences reside on the other side of our apprehensions. The fear of failure can lead to the satisfaction of accomplishment. The fear of the unknown can reveal uncharted territories of growth. The fear of rejection can pave the way to authentic connections, and the fear of success can unlock the doors to our fullest potential.

Music Reference: *Hans Zimmer –*
Time from *Inception* (2010)

The music that captures this delicate balance between fear

and courage is Hans Zimmer's **Time** from the film *Inception*. The slow, building progression of the track reflects the journey of facing our fears. It starts softly, almost hesitantly, much like the quiet fears we hold within us. But as the track progresses, it grows more intense, symbolizing the strength and courage required to confront the uncertainties of life. By the time it reaches its crescendo, it mirrors the emotional release that comes when we embrace fear, pushing through it to discover the richness of life on the other side.

The haunting beauty of Zimmer's composition evokes the emotional depth of our struggles with fear and the ultimate triumph of facing them. As you listen to **Time**, let it remind you that, much like the characters in *Inception*, we often must navigate the layers of our own mind to find the courage to act.

Hans Zimmer – Time is available on Spotify, Apple Music, and YouTube. Its relevance to this chapter is in its portrayal of the gradual realization that fear, when confronted, leads to personal growth and transformation. Society often encourages us to avoid fear at all costs, to seek comfort and safety above all else. But what if we reframed our relationship with fear? What if we saw it not as an adversary to be defeated but as a guide, illuminating the path to a life truly lived?

Fear is experienced differently across cultures and genders. In some cultures, fear of bringing shame to the family can be a powerful force that shapes life decisions, while in others, the fear of not achieving personal success might be more prevalent. Women might face fears related to personal safety or societal judgment in ways that men do not. Understanding how these fears are culturally and socially constructed can help you address them in a way that is both personally meaningful and contextually appropriate.

To confront the fear of our lives is to embrace vulnerability. It is to recognize that life's most meaningful moments are often the result of taking risks, of stepping into the unknown with open hearts and minds. It's about understanding that the journey is not meant to be free of fear but to be enriched by it.

Expanded Practical Reflection

Now that we've explored the concept of fear, take a moment to reflect on your own life:

Reflection

- What fears have held you back from pursuing the life you truly want?
- Are there opportunities that you've missed because of fear?
  Write down three fears that have limited your potential. Next to each one, identify an action—no matter how small—you can take to face it.

Exercise

For the next seven days, commit to confronting one small fear each day. This could be something as simple as initiating a difficult conversation or taking a step toward a long-held goal. Document how you feel after each day. Notice how your relationship with fear begins to shift as you face it directly.

As you reflect on your own life, consider the fears that may have held you back, the dreams that remain unfulfilled, and the possibilities that lie just beyond your comfort zone. Remember that you are not alone in your fears; they are a universal part of the human experience.

So, I invite you to ask yourself, *Are you afraid of your life?* And when you do, may you find the courage to answer with a resounding, *No, I am not afraid. I am alive, and I am ready to embrace every moment, fear and all.*

The Psychology of Fear

Fear is a powerful emotion rooted in our brain's survival mechanisms, specifically the fight-or-flight response governed by the amygdala. While this response was crucial for our ancestors, today it often overreacts to perceived threats, creating anxiety and avoidance behaviours. Childhood experiences, such as overprotective parenting or early trauma, can amplify these fears in adulthood. Cognitive-behavioural techniques, such as exposure therapy and cognitive restructuring, can help us reframe our fears and reduce their impact on our lives. By understanding the psychology behind fear, we can begin to confront and overcome it.

Conclusion

Fear can be a formidable force, but understanding it is the key to unlocking our potential and living more fully.

Whether it's stepping into the unknown like Truman or confronting the layers of our subconscious like in *Inception*, fear is a natural part of the journey to self-discovery. The decision to confront it, rather than avoid it, will ultimately define how fully we experience life.

Film:
The Truman Show (1998)

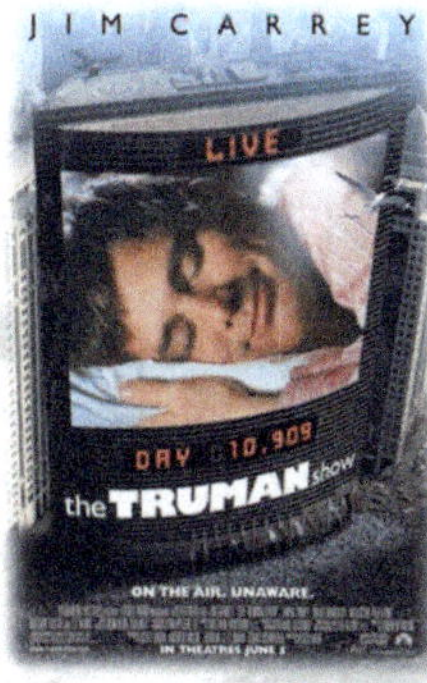

Platforms: Netflix, Amazon Prime, Apple TV+

Story Relevance: The film explores themes of fear, control, and the courage to break free from a false reality, mirroring the journey of confronting fear in this chapter.

Music:
Hans Zimmer
Time from *Inception* (2010)

Platforms: Spotify, Apple Music, YouTube

Story Relevance: The track's gradual build-up and emotional crescendo represent the journey of confronting and overcoming fear, making it an ideal soundtrack for this chapter.

Chapter 16

Do You Trust yourself?

Trust is a thread that weaves through every experience and interaction, but do we trust ourselves?

Trust in oneself is a profound and often overlooked aspect of personal growth and fulfilment. It's a question we must all confront on our journey through life: *Do you trust yourself?*

At times, it may feel like life is an intricate puzzle, and we are the ones holding the missing pieces. We seek validation from external sources—family, friends, society—when the true key to understanding lies within. Trusting oneself is not about arrogance or blind self-confidence; it's about acknowledging your own wisdom, intuition, and capacity to make decisions that align with your values and aspirations.

Film Reference:
Good Will Hunting (1997)

In the film *Good Will Hunting*, the character Will, played by Matt Damon, is a brilliant young man working as a janitor at MIT. Though gifted with extraordinary intellect, he struggles with self-trust, masking his insecurities behind a tough exterior and refusing to accept the opportunities that his talents afford him. Through therapy with Sean (Robin Williams), Will slowly learns to trust himself—his intelligence, his emotions, and his worth—ultimately realizing that his fear of vulnerability has kept him from living up to his full potential.

This narrative aligns with the core theme of this chapter: trusting oneself. Will's journey shows that self-trust is not just about recognizing your talents, but about embracing your vulnerabilities, acknowledging your past traumas, and trusting that you are capable of healing and growth.

Good Will Hunting is available on Netflix, Amazon Prime, and Apple TV+. Its relevance to this chapter lies in its exploration of self-trust, vulnerability, and the journey toward personal growth through self-compassion and self-awareness.

Trusting oneself is not always easy, especially when life throws uncertainties our way. So, how do you know if you truly trust yourself? Here are some reflections to consider:

1. Trust Begins with Self-Compassion

Are you kind and forgiving toward yourself, especially in moments of failure or doubt? Self-compassion allows you to bounce back from setbacks, knowing that you are deserving of love and understanding, just as much as anyone else. Like Will Hunting, we all carry wounds from our past. Learning to trust yourself begins with treating those wounds with kindness, not judgment.

2. Intuition - Your Compass

Do you listen to that inner voice, or do you silence it in favour of external opinions? Trusting yourself means honouring your intuition and allowing it to shape your choices. In *Good Will Hunting,* Will learns that his intuition and emotions are not weaknesses but sources of strength. Trusting yourself means knowing when to follow that inner compass.

Self-awareness helps us navigate life confidently.
When faced with decisions, do you second-guess yourself or trust your judgment?
Trusting yourself means making choices with conviction, even when outcomes are uncertain.

Music Reference: *Cry Little Sister* from *The Lost Boys* (1987)

The haunting and soulful melody of **Cry Little Sister**, from ***The Lost Boys***, captures the deep internal struggle between darkness and self-realization, echoing the theme of self-trust in this chapter. The song's melancholic tone reflects the emotional tension of trusting oneself despite fear and doubt. Like the protagonists in *The Lost Boys*, we face battles between what we fear and who we know we can become.

Movie	Soundtrack	Scan QR code
The Lost Boys	**Cry Little Sister**	

The lyrics of the song - "**Thou shalt not fear**" - serve as a powerful reminder that fear is often what holds us back from trusting ourselves. This track's gothic tone, layered with haunting vocals, represents the internal battles we fight when faced with choices that test our self-confidence. Ultimately, the song underscores the strength we find when we finally embrace ourselves, imperfections and all, and take ownership of our choices. Its relevance to this chapter lies in its exploration of inner conflict and the journey toward self-trust, making it a perfect soundtrack for moments of deep reflection and personal growth.

4. Fear and Doubt are Natural Companions

Do fear and doubt often cloud your judgment? Trust is not the absence of fear but the ability to move forward despite it. Recognize that fear and doubt are natural companions on life's journey, but they need not be the drivers of your decisions.

5. Honesty with Yourself is Crucial

Are you honest with yourself about your desires, dreams, and limitations? Trusting yourself requires honesty. It means acknowledging your authentic self and embracing your imperfections as part of what makes you unique.

6. Embrace Change and Personal Growth

Do you trust yourself enough to embrace change and personal growth? Trusting yourself means having faith in your ability to adapt, learn, and evolve as you move through life. Just as Will Hunting learns to break free from the shackles of his past, trusting yourself means letting go of limiting beliefs and stepping into your potential.

Take a moment to reflect on your relationship with self-trust:

Reflection

- Do you often second-guess your decisions, or do you trust your intuition and judgment?

- Reflect on a time when you trusted yourself fully—what was the outcome? Now, think of a time when you doubted yourself. What was the impact?

Exercise

For the next week, practice trusting yourself by making decisions without seeking external validation. Begin with small choices, like what to eat or how to spend your free time. Gradually build up to more significant decisions. Journal about the experience, noting how you felt when you trusted your intuition and whether you felt more aligned with your values.

Conclusion

Self-trust is not something that comes easily—it's something we cultivate over time through self-awareness, self-compassion, and the willingness to embrace both our strengths and weaknesses. In *Good Will Hunting*, Will's journey from self-doubt to self-trust is not just a personal triumph but a reminder that true growth comes from within. Similarly, *Cry Little Sister* from *The Lost Boys* reflects the inner conflict of fear, but also the ultimate power of trusting oneself to overcome the darkness.

PART 6: EXPLORATION

We shall explore connections such as mother's unconditional love, the impact of solitude on mental health, self-renewal and benefits of slowing life down.

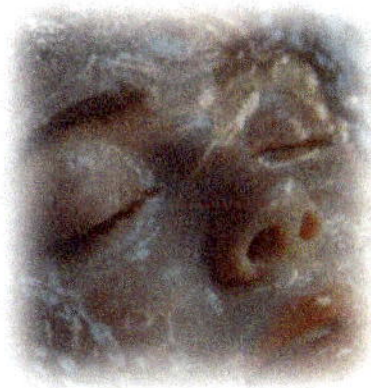

Chapter 17 **Embracing Infinities**
Examines the concept of infinity as it manifests in emotions, connections, and experiences, illustrated by mother's infinite love, and connections.
Mother's Love and Beyond
Infinities in Everyday Life
Relatable Music

Chapter 18 **Does Isolation Help?**
Reflects on the role of solitude in personal growth, examining how isolation can serve as a space for self-reflection, resilience, and clarity
Intention
Balance
The Effects of Isolation on Mental Health

Chapter 19 **Coming Up for Air**
Explores the importance of disconnecting from daily pressures to find moments of renewal, emphasizing how embracing silence, slowing down, and stepping back can enhance well-being.
Disconnect
Embracing Silence
Slowing Down

Chapter 17

Embracing Infinities

Mother's Love and Beyond

In a world where so much feels finite—our time, our resources, our energy - there exists something awe-inspiring: the concept of infinity. While we often think of infinity as an *abstract mathematical* idea, it manifests in the most intimate parts of our lives. Infinity isn't just a number that stretches beyond comprehension; it's present in our emotions, our connections, and the depth of our experiences. And perhaps the most powerful example of infinity in our everyday lives is the *unquantifiable, boundless* love of a mother.

Mother's love is often described as *unconditional*, but a more fitting word might be infinite. It doesn't stop at birth, or in childhood, or even in adulthood. It extends beyond the physical, transcending time and space, unyielding and eternal. This love is an anchor that we carry with us through every stage of life, and even when a mother is no longer present, her love remains - a force that continues to guide, protect, and nurture.

Film Reference: *Interstellar* (2014)

In the film *Interstellar*, this concept of infinite love is explored on a cosmic scale. Dr. Brand, played by Anne Hathaway, speaks powerfully about how love defies the boundaries of time and space. She suggests that love, much like gravity, is a force beyond explanation—an idea that echoes the immeasurable love of a mother.

The protagonist, Cooper, embarks on a journey across galaxies driven by his love for his daughter, Murph. Decades pass, and light-years stretch between them, but his love remains constant, pulling him back to her. This film serves as a reminder that some connections are so profound, so infinite, that they transcend the finite limitations of life.

Interstellar is available on Netflix, Amazon Prime, and Apple TV+. The film's exploration of love as an infinite force ties directly to this chapter's theme—reminding us that some relationships and emotions are boundless, enduring through time and space.

Infinities in Everyday Life

While a mother's love is a universal example, we encounter other infinities in our daily lives. Moments of pure joy, the vastness of the night sky, the depths of our dreams—these are reflections of the boundless nature of human existence.

In the small, fleeting moments, we experience infinities: a song that stirs emotions from decades past, a memory that transports us back in time, or words spoken that echo in our minds long after they've been said. These moments, though brief, carry an infinite weight that stretches beyond time and place. They remind us that while so much of life is finite, certain experiences, emotions, and connections reach beyond all limits.

Relatable Music

Youn Sun Nah - "Voyage"

Youn Sun Nah's *"Voyage"* is a reflective, ethereal piece that captures the feeling of embarking on an emotional journey—much like the infinite voyage of love, self-discovery, and life itself. The haunting tones and soft vocal delivery evoke a sense of introspection and infinite wonder, inviting the listener to delve into the unknown and embrace the emotional depth that life offers.

Artist	Song	Scan QR code
Youn Sun Nah	Yoyage	

Music: Relevance: The ethereal beauty of this piece reflects the infinite nature of emotional journeys, mirroring the boundless aspects of love and life.

Life is a story woven with complex themes of adventure, courage, and introspection, much like *Scheherazade: The Young Prince.*

Each note is a step into a vast world of endless possibilities, inviting us to embrace the richness of life's unfolding tale.

Movie	Soundtrack	Scan QR code
Rimsky Korsakov	Scheherazade	

The Infinite Nature of Legacy

Just as a mother's love can extend far beyond her physical presence, so too can the impact we have on others. The legacies we leave behind—whether through our actions, our words, or our relationships—are another reflection of infinity. We may not live forever, but the love we give, the kindness we show, and the impact we have on others can ripple outward, infinitely. Like the waves of a stone dropped into a pond, the echoes of our existence extend far beyond what we can see.

Consider the love passed down from generation to generation. It's not a love that diminishes over time but rather one that compounds, growing richer as it is nurtured, shared, and re-experienced in new forms. The love a mother gives her children becomes the foundation for the love they give to their own families, continuing the cycle of infinity.

Reflection and Practical Takeaway

As you think about the infinities in your own life, ask yourself:

- **What relationships in your life feel infinite?** Think about the people whose love or impact transcends time and distance. How do these connections shape who you are?

- **Where do you see infinities in your everyday moments?** Is it in the smile of a loved one, the beauty of a sunset, or the depth of a favourite song? Take time to appreciate these boundless experiences that enrich your life.

- **What legacy are you leaving behind?** Consider how your actions today will shape the world tomorrow. How can you nurture infinite love, kindness, or generosity in your relationships and the world around you?

Conclusion

In a world filled with limits, embracing the infinities of life can offer us a sense of peace and fulfilment.

Whether it's the endless depth of a mother's love, the infinite potential in a single moment of connection, or the legacies that stretch far beyond our time, we are surrounded by boundless experiences.

So, the next time you feel overwhelmed by the pressures of time or the constraints of life, remember the infinities that exist within and around you.

These are the forces that transcend the ordinary and remind us that while much in life is fleeting, love, connection, and impact are infinite.

Chapter 18

Does Isolation Help?

Is retreating into a cocoon of solitude the key to self-discovery, or does it hold us back? Does isolation light our path or cast shadows over our progress? The blankets of darkness we create can only be pieced by headlamps we decide to switch on. Often, we find ourselves at a crossroads, with isolation stepping into the spotlight.

Isolation, at its core, can be a double-edged sword. On one hand, it offers a respite from the noise and demands of the external world. It provides a sanctuary for introspection, self-reflection, and the nurturing of creativity. It can be a space for healing and rejuvenation, an escape from the relentless pace of life. Many great thinkers, writers, and artists have sought solitude to tap into their inner wellsprings of inspiration.

Relatable Music

In times of solitude, we often find a deeper connection to ourselves. *The Lonely Shepherd* evokes the quiet beauty of isolation, where reflection and peace can be found, but only after embracing the stillness within.

Composer	Composition	Scan QR code
Gheorghe Zamfir	The Lonely Shepherd	

On the other hand, isolation, when prolonged or chosen for the wrong reasons, can become a self-imposed prison. It can lead to loneliness, stagnation, and a distorted view of reality. It might inadvertently distance us from the very experiences, relationships, and growth opportunities that make life rich and meaningful. Isolation can amplify feelings of depression, anxiety, and disconnection.

In African philosophy, Ubuntu offers a counter-narrative to isolation. Ubuntu, often translated as "I am because we are," emphasizes that our identity and humanity are shaped by our relationships with others. While solitude can foster self-reflection, Ubuntu teaches that we are intrinsically social beings. True personal growth happens not in isolation but in community. As the saying goes, "A person is a person through other people." In this way, isolation can be beneficial only if it ultimately brings us back to deeper connection with the world.

In many Indigenous cultures, particularly among Native American tribes, isolation is often used as a time to reconnect with nature, not to escape from life, but to deepen one's relationship with the earth. Nature is seen as a living being, a teacher that offers wisdom and guidance. Solitude in the wilderness is an opportunity for spiritual reflection and renewal, but it is also a reminder that we are part of a larger ecosystem, interconnected with all living things. This perspective suggests that isolation can be transformative when it brings us closer to the natural world.

The film ***Into the Wild***, based on the true story of Christopher McCandless, explores the profound impact of isolation. After abandoning his family and possessions, McCandless ventures into the wilderness of Alaska, seeking freedom and self-discovery. His journey into isolation was meant to help him reconnect with nature and himself, free from the materialism and distractions of society. However,

the film highlights the dangers of prolonged isolation. As McCandless distances himself from human connection, he begins to realize the cost of his solitude.
Ultimately, his revelation—"Happiness is only real when shared" - shows that while isolation can provide clarity, prolonged detachment from meaningful relationships can lead to tragic outcomes.

This film serves as a cautionary tale about the balance between solitude and connection, reminding us that isolation, while a powerful tool for personal growth, should not come at the expense of human connection.

Its relevance to this chapter lies in its exploration of isolation as both a means of self-discovery and a potential path to despair when taken too far.

So, how do we discern whether isolation is a helpful ally or a treacherous foe in our journey through life? Here are some reflections:

Intention
Consider the intention behind your isolation. Are you seeking solitude for self-care, reflection, or creative pursuits, or is it a way to escape from discomfort or avoid facing life's challenges? The intention behind isolation often shapes its impact.

Balance is key.
While moments of solitude can be nourishing, prolonged isolation may lead to a sense of disconnection. It's essential to strike a balance between time alone and time spent with others, fostering both inner growth and external connections.

Music Reference: *Sound of Silence* by Simon & Garfunkel (1964)

The iconic song *Sound of Silence* by Simon & Garfunkel encapsulates the haunting effects of isolation. The song's lyrics speak to the experience of feeling alone in a crowded world, where disconnection from others leads to a kind of metaphorical silence. It reflects the internal struggle of isolation—the tension between wanting solitude and fearing the resulting loneliness. "Hello darkness, my old friend" symbolizes how isolation can become both a comfort and a curse. As the song builds, the sense of alienation deepens, mirroring the emotional impact prolonged isolation can have on mental and emotional well-being. This song underscores the importance of understanding isolation's role in our lives. It reminds us that while silence and solitude can foster deep introspection, they can also lead to feelings of disconnection and sorrow if not balanced with meaningful social interaction.

Sound of Silence by Simon & Garfunkel is available on Spotify, Apple Music, and YouTube. Its relevance to this chapter is its reflection on the emotional weight of isolation, offering a powerful reminder of the importance of connection amidst solitude.

3. Self-Reflection

Use isolation as a tool for self-reflection and self-discovery. It can be an opportunity to gain clarity on your values, goals, and desires. However, be mindful not to spiral into rumination or self-criticism.

4. Connection

Recognize the importance of human connection. We are social beings, and our well-being often thrives when we engage in meaningful relationships. Isolation should not become a barrier to nurturing these connections.

5. Goals

Define your goals for isolation. What do you hope to achieve during this time? Having clear objectives can help you make the most of your solitude.

Isolation, like many aspects of life, is a nuanced experience. It can be a helpful tool when used intentionally and in moderation. It can provide moments of insight, creativity, and rejuvenation. However, it's vital to be mindful of the potential pitfalls of excessive isolation and to ensure that it serves your overall well-being and personal growth.

The Effects of Isolation on Mental Health

Isolation can have profound effects on mental health, both positive and negative. While solitude may foster self-reflection and creativity, prolonged isolation—especially when involuntary- can lead to depression, anxiety, and cognitive decline.

We thrive on social interaction, and without it, cognitive functions can deteriorate. Studies show that isolation increases the risk of mental health issues, particularly in older adults. Whether chosen or imposed, isolation's impact is shaped by various cultural, social, and economic factors.

In rural or economically disadvantaged communities, physical isolation is often a daily reality due to limited access to transportation and services. Conversely, in urban areas, social isolation can occur despite close physical proximity, as the fast-paced, individualistic nature of city life fosters emotional distance. Cultural expectations, such as traditional gender roles that confine women to the home, can also contribute to isolation and limit social interaction.

Recognizing these diverse influences helps us better understand and navigate our own experiences with isolation.

Conclusion

Ultimately, whether isolation serves as a tool for growth or a barrier to well-being depends on how you engage with it. By understanding the factors that shape our experience of isolation, we can better navigate its complexities. Both solitude and connection are integral to life's journey—each offering unique lessons. Embrace them in harmony and settle with a personalized form of enrichment that feels right for you and no one else.

Relatable Music

Music: *Sound of Silence* by Simon & Garfunkel (1964)

The song captures the emotional weight of isolation and disconnection, reinforcing the chapter's message about balancing solitude with meaningful connection.

Artist	Title	Scan QR code
The Sound of Silence	***Simon & Garfunkel***	

In the quiet moments of solitude, when the world seems distant, we often find ourselves confronting the most vulnerable parts of our being.

Children of the Night captures this feeling—speaking to the hearts of those who navigate life's darker, more introspective periods.

Artist	Title	Scan QR code
The Jones Girls	**Children of the Night**	

Chapter 19

Coming Up for Air

In the relentless pursuit of our dreams and the grind of daily life, we often find ourselves submerged in a sea of responsibilities, ambitions, and a growing task list. It's as if

we've been holding our breath, diving ever deeper into the currents of life, barely pausing to resurface and breathe. But every journey has a moment when we must come up for air, whether we've planned it or not. Countless moments, each with their own color and feel, make up our lives.

Yet, in our drive to accomplish, to achieve, and to keep pace, we risk losing sight of the beauty in simply being present. When did going for a walk, calling an old friend, or watching the sun set become things we "schedule"?

We forget the importance of pausing, of reconnecting with ourselves, with the world, and with the people who matter.

Coming up for air isn't about giving up on dreams. It's about refreshing our vision and ensuring we're still on the path that feels true. It's a reminder that the journey of life isn't solely about reaching the destination but about experiencing every step along the way. It's about finding stillness amid chaos, gratitude in the face of challenges, and wonder in the everyday.

In these pauses, we get to reconnect with what sustains us. Sometimes, it's a walk in the park, maybe with a dog who

understands life's joys better than most of us. Or it's those moments when we're outdoors—watching waves roll in or listening to the soft rustle of leaves overhead—that remind us of a rhythm that's older, deeper, and gentler than our schedules and deadlines. And as we savour these moments, we find ourselves more present for others, more attuned to the needs of those around us.

As we rise from life's undertows, we often glimpse moments of peace and renewal - like the gentle tones in Ella Fitzgerald's *Summertime*, where we emerge from the storm to find ourselves in sunlight, unburdened by past struggles. In those notes, we're reminded that coming up for air is not merely an escape; it's a way to savour the journey and to see it anew.

Artist	Title	Scan QR code
Ella Fitzgerald	**Summertime**	

As you pause to come up for air, life, once overwhelming, becomes clearer and more navigable. You rediscover the joy of being present, the power of stillness, and the wisdom that's been quietly waiting within. In these moments, you find not only sustenance but also the inspiration and strength to continue your journey with renewed purpose and clarity.

Take a deep breath and allow yourself to come up for air. Embrace the beauty of each moment, for it is in these pauses that the true essence of life is revealed.

Disconnect

Unplug from the digital world now and then.

Step away from screens and social media, silencing the distractions that can drown out your inner voice.

Embrace Silence

In the midst of life's noise, seek out moments of silence. Silence can be a powerful teacher, allowing you to listen to your own wisdom and hear the subtler rhythms of the world around you.

As this chapter closes, consider not only coming up for air but also consciously slowing down. There is beauty, even harmony, in letting the world's pace recede. In slowing down, we discover that life's worth lies not only in movement but in moments of stillness - a cadence that offers space to breathe and truly see.

Slowing Down

There's a moment when the world seems to pause—the soft hush of early morning fog over the water or the first glimmer of sunlight breaking through the trees. In that silence, we realize that success isn't always found in grand achievements but in the quiet pauses we take along the way. In this space, a simple walk becomes an invitation to listen, to reconnect, to breathe.

We spend so much of life reaching for goals, but there's an art to appreciating what's already around us. ***Loose Ends'*** soulful rhythm in *"**Slow Down**"* captures that essence perfectly, inviting us to take a step back and savour what's here now.

Artist	**Title**	**Scan QR code**
Loose ends	***Slow down***	

Slowing down allows us to find beauty in the unremarkable: the stillness of a wooded path, the song of a bird, the open horizon. These moments remind us that life's worth is found in more than what we produce or accomplish. They speak to a deeper part of us, where fulfilment is found not in movement, but in rest. In slowing down, we allow ourselves to connect—not just with nature, but with people, our communities, and even the memories we carry. This isn't an escape from life but a fuller embrace of it. It's a chance to step back, to savour, to simply be.

As you read this, consider your own moments of pause. Let them be as vital as your pursuits. Perhaps, like the cadence of a favourite song, they can offer a rhythm to your life that's richer, slower, and more sustaining.

PART 7: EMOTIONAL CROSSROADS

In this section, we examine transformative experiences that test our resilience, self-sufficiency, and sense of purpose in the face of troubles.

Chapter 20 **Uncharted Territory**
Explores the unknown aspects of our emotional landscape, encouraging readers to navigate new emotional depths and challenges with openness and courage.
Uncertainty
Relatable Music
Emotional Intelligence and Regulation
Practical Advice

Chapter 21 **Living Many Lives in One Lifetime**
Examines the idea of reinvention and embracing various phases of life, inviting readers to reflect on the possibility of evolving through multiple identities and roles.
The Art of Reinvention
The Power of Letting Go
Rebirth Through Reinvention
The Lives We Live Through Others
The Complexity of Multiple Lives
Leaving a Legacy of Lives Lived

Chapter 22 **Self-Sufficiency – Road to Recovery**
Discusses the journey toward self-reliance, resilience, and recovery, offering insights into overcoming adversity and finding strength within.
Relatable Music

Chapter 20

Uncharted Territory

Life's journey is often likened to a grand adventure, a voyage into the unknown. But there is one territory within this vast landscape that is perhaps the most uncharted, the most complex, and the most bewildering: our own emotional terrain.

Emotions, like the ever-shifting tides of the sea, can carry us to places of profound beauty and serenity, or they can thrust us into tempestuous waters fraught with turmoil and uncertainty. Our emotional landscape is a vast expanse of unexplored territory and navigating it can be both exhilarating and daunting.

This emotional terrain is where we experience the full spectrum of human feelings—joy, sorrow, love, anger, fear, and everything in between. Shaped by our past experiences, our present circumstances, and our hopes and fears for the future, it is constantly evolving. Yet, despite the profound impact emotions have on our lives, many of us remain strangers in this uncharted territory. We suppress feelings, deny their existence, or allow them to control our actions without truly understanding their origins or purpose.

So, how can we navigate this vast emotional landscape with grace and wisdom? It starts with a deep sense of self-awareness.

The journey begins with recognizing and acknowledging your emotions as they arise. Name them and sit with them without judgment. Emotions are messengers, and understanding their source can be the first step toward clarity and healing.

Embrace vulnerability as a pathway to emotional connection. It takes courage to share your feelings with others, but doing so can lead to deeper relationships and a more profound understanding of yourself.

Uncertainty

Life often leads us into unfamiliar emotional places, where old coping mechanisms no longer serve us, and where we face the unknown with nothing but our feelings to guide us. This can feel disorienting, but it is precisely in these moments of uncertainty that true transformation begins.

One powerful example of this journey can be seen in the film ***"Eat Pray Love"***. Based on the memoir by Elizabeth Gilbert, this film follows the protagonist's quest for self-discovery after she decides to leave behind a life that no longer fulfils her.

The film poignantly captures the essence of letting go of the familiar—whether it be a marriage or a routine life—to explore uncharted emotional and physical territory. It is a journey not just across countries, but across the landscape of her own heart. The emotional depth of the film illustrates the courage it takes to step into the unknown, and the rewards of finding peace and joy in one's own company. Like Gilbert's journey, embracing the uncertainty in your own life can lead to profound emotional and spiritual growth.

In music, few pieces evoke the complexity of emotions and the journey through uncertainty as powerfully as ***Beethoven's Symphony No. 9.*** The final movement, famously known as **"Ode to Joy,"** begins with a sense of tension and struggle before swelling into one of the most triumphant, joyful melodies in all classical music. Beethoven composed this piece during a time of personal hardship, having lost his hearing completely, yet the symphony represents triumph over adversity, the ultimate expression of joy and human resilience. As you navigate your own emotional terrain, listening to this powerful symphony can remind you that, just as the music transitions from chaos to clarity, so too can your emotional journey lead to a place of joy and fulfilment.

Have you ever clung to someone or something out of comfort, even when deep down you knew it was time to let go? Perhaps you stayed because the thought of starting over seemed too overwhelming, or maybe you were afraid of what you would find on the other side. Trust me, I've been there. We all have. But here's what I've learned from navigating these emotional landscapes: the real power lies in releasing what no longer serves us.

The journey through uncharted emotional territory isn't about finding a map or a clear path. It's about trusting that you have everything you need within yourself to move forward. When you hold on to things—whether it's a relationship, a job, or a belief system—that no longer supports your growth, you're denying yourself the opportunity to explore what could be. Letting go is hard, no doubt. It feels like stepping into the unknown with nothing but faith in yourself. But it's also freeing.

When you release these attachments, you make space for new emotions, new experiences, and new parts of yourself to emerge. You begin to discover strengths and capabilities you didn't know you had. More importantly, you learn that you can thrive in your own company, that you can find joy not in what you hold onto, but in what you let go of.

So, if you find yourself stuck in a space that feels stagnant or suffocating, it's time to step into the unknown. Trust that in this emotional wilderness, you will find not just a path forward, but a stronger, more resilient version of yourself. Remember, it's in the unknown that we discover our true power.

Relatable Music

In moments of uncertainty, subtle whispers and exchanges can guide us forward. Just as in Mozart's *Sull'aria*, delicate yet profound connections offer solace and direction when venturing into the unknown.

Artist	Title	Scan QR code
Mozart	Le nozze di Figaro	

Emotional Intelligence and Regulation

Navigating uncharted emotional territory requires more than just awareness; it demands emotional intelligence (EQ). EQ involves recognizing, understanding, and managing your own emotions while empathizing with others.

At the centre of our emotional responses is the limbic system, particularly the amygdala, which governs our initial emotional reactions. However, it is the prefrontal cortex that helps regulate these emotions, allowing us to process them thoughtfully rather than react impulsively. Developing emotional regulation strategies, such as mindfulness, journaling, and cognitive-behavioural techniques, can help you respond to emotional challenges with resilience and clarity.

Mindfulness practices allow you to observe emotions without being swept away by them, giving you the space to respond rather than react. Journaling serves as a release, a way to process complex emotions by giving them structure and clarity on paper.

Cognitive-behavioural strategies help you reframe negative thought patterns, allowing you to challenge distorted thinking and regain control over emotional responses.

Exploring new emotional territory can be particularly daunting for those from cultural or familial backgrounds where emotional expression is discouraged. In many cultures, men are taught to suppress vulnerability, while women may feel the pressure to prioritize the emotions of others over their own.

Additionally, individuals from marginalized communities often face emotional burdens related to discrimination or societal exclusion.

Understanding these diverse experiences is essential as you navigate your own emotional journey, ensuring that your path is informed by both personal and cultural understanding.

Practical Advice for Navigating Emotional Territory

Embrace Vulnerability
All too often perceived as a weakness, but it is a powerful gateway to deeper emotional connection and self-discovery. Sharing your true feelings, even when it's uncomfortable, can help you form more genuine relationships with others and with yourself. Lean into the discomfort of being vulnerable; it's through this openness that we grow.

Practice Mindfulness to Anchor Yourself
In uncharted emotional waters, mindfulness serves as an anchor. Take a few moments each day to sit quietly, focusing on your breath or the present moment. By grounding yourself in mindfulness, you create space between your emotional reactions and the actions you take. This helps you navigate turbulent feelings with clarity rather than impulsiveness.

Acknowledge Emotional Triggers
Understanding what triggers your emotional responses are essential for navigating emotional territory. Keep a journal to track situations, people, or thoughts that spark strong emotions. With greater awareness, you can respond rather

than react when those triggers arise, transforming emotional challenges into opportunities for growth.

Cultivate Emotional Resilience

Emotional resilience isn't about avoiding pain—it's about learning to adapt and grow through it. Life will inevitably bring challenges, but each one is an opportunity to build resilience. Recognize that even the most painful emotions, like grief or anger, can be powerful catalysts for transformation.

Use Cognitive Behavioural Techniques to Manage Overwhelm

When emotions become overwhelming, cognitive-behavioural strategies can help reframe your thoughts. Ask yourself, "Is my reaction proportionate to the situation?" and "What evidence do I have to support this feeling?" By challenging automatic negative thoughts, you can regain control over how you respond emotionally.

Reflection often brings us back to simpler, wistful times. *On Days Like These* reminds us of the beauty in fleeting moments when life feels slow and nostalgic, as we reflect on the choices and experiences that define our journey.

Artist	Title	Scan QR code
Matt Munro	**On Days Like These**	

Chapter 21

Living Many Lives in One Lifetime

As the old saying goes: "***You only live once.***"

Biologically, yes but if you explore beyond physical, we realize that most of us go through significant transitions that feel like a completely different life many times.

The person we were at 20 is not the same as the one we are at 40, and by the time we reach 60 or beyond, we've shed so many layers of our former selves that it's as if we've lived multiple lifetimes—each with its own stories, triumphs, failures, and rebirths.

The Art of Reinvention

Reinvention can feel like an *unfinished symphony*. We may never fully resolve all the notes, and the melody of our lives shifts with each new experience. *Unfinished Sympathy* by Massive Attack captures this sense of emotional evolution - there's a depth to it that echoes the unfinished nature of our personal journeys.

Artist	Title	Scan QR code
Massive attack	***Unfinished symphony***	

Reinvention doesn't come with a clear conclusion; it's a work in progress, an ongoing composition, where each shift and change become part of a larger, evolving piece.

Our priorities shift, our relationships change, and the dreams that once defined us may no longer feel relevant. In the process of living, we continually reinvent ourselves—often without even realizing it.

Pharrell Williams' *Happy* is a perfect anthem for the art of reinvention because it encourages us to embrace joy, even when life's direction seems unclear.

Artist	Title	Scan QR code
Happy	***Pharrell Williams***	

Reinvention isn't about waiting for everything to make sense—it's about dancing to the beat, even if you're not entirely sure what the tune is. As Pharrell reminds us, clapping along through life's twists and turns is sometimes the best way to keep moving forward.

Another powerful example of this reinvention can be found in ***The Curious Case of Benjamin Button***. Benjamin, who ages in reverse, experiences life in an entirely unique way. Each stage of his life unfolds with a new perspective, offering him the chance to live multiple lives within one lifetime. As we watch him navigate these phases, we're reminded that life isn't linear—it's full of unexpected turns, moments of transformation, and opportunities to reinvent ourselves, just as Benjamin does. In our youth, we are driven by possibility, chasing the futures we've envisioned. We pour ourselves into relationships, careers, and experiences with the belief that they will shape who we are. But as we move through life, we encounter moments of transformation—sometimes subtle, sometimes seismic—

that force us to step into a new version of ourselves.
This is the nature of living multiple lives within one lifetime. Each phase, each version of ourselves, is a chapter that contributes to the larger story of who we are. And with each reinvention, we gain new perspectives, deeper wisdom, and a clearer sense of what truly matters.

The Power of Letting Go

To fully embrace the concept of living many lives, we must first learn to let go. Letting go of the people we once were, the identities we built, and the definitions we clung to. This isn't about denying our pasts but about recognizing that we are constantly evolving. Who we were at 25 doesn't have to define who we are at 50. The career we thought we'd pursue forever may not be the one that fulfils us in later years. The relationships that shaped us in one chapter may not be the ones that carry us through the next.

Letting go is hard. We invest so much of ourselves in our careers, relationships, and dreams that it feels like failure when they no longer serve us. But letting go is not an act of giving up—it's an act of growth. It allows us to step into the next phase of our lives with an open heart and a willingness to embrace new possibilities.
Each version of us has value, and each chapter brings lessons that enrich the ones that follow. The key is to carry forward what we've learned and to release what no longer aligns with who we are becoming.

Rebirth Through Reinvention

Living multiple lives means embracing the art of reinvention. Society often pressures us to be consistent, to stick to one path, to follow the script. But life is far more dynamic than that. We are not static beings, and we are not defined by a single narrative. We are constantly changing, learning, and evolving.

Reinvention is a gift. It allows us to pivot, to rediscover passions we once buried, to chase new dreams, and to redefine success and happiness. It gives us the freedom to live a life that reflects our truest selves, even if that self has changed over time.

The most successful people, the most fulfilled people, are those who embrace reinvention. They understand that living multiple lives isn't a departure from who they are—it's an expansion of their potential. It's a deepening of their understanding of what it means to live fully, without the constraints of societal expectations.

The Lives We Live Through Others

Our lives are not only defined by our personal experiences but also by the people we share them with. Every meaningful relationship brings with it a new life, a new perspective, a new way of seeing the world. Whether it's through friendship, love, or parenthood, the lives we live through others are just as transformative as the lives we live for ourselves.

When we love deeply, we are changed. We live the experiences of those we care for, adopting their joys, their struggles, and their dreams as part of our own journey.

Parenthood, in particular, is one of the most profound lives we can live. When we become parents, we are no longer living solely for ourselves. We are entrusted with the growth of another life, and in doing so, we experience a life that is intertwined with theirs, marked by sacrifice, growth, and boundless love.

The song ***Landslide*** by **Fleetwood Mac** captures this theme of evolving through life's changes and relationships. The lyrics, "Can I handle the seasons of my life?" echo the journey of living multiple lives and coming to terms with the inevitable transformations we go through. The song's poignant reflection on change and self-discovery resonates with the central idea that life is constantly shifting, and with each shift, we are reborn. (Available on Spotify, Apple Music, and YouTube.)

The Complexity of Multiple Lives

Living several lives within one lifetime isn't a linear journey. There are moments when the past versions of us overlap with the present. We carry forward the lessons, traumas, and triumphs of our former selves as we continue to evolve. The paths we take can sometimes seem contradictory, as if the person we are today would hardly recognize the person we were years ago. And yet, every life we live is interconnected.

The beauty of living multiple lives is that we are not bound by one single definition of who we are. The career we pursued in our 20s doesn't have to be the one we end with in our 60s. The relationship that defined us for a decade may fade, making space for new connections that reflect our current selves. Another powerful soundtrack that captures the essence of reinvention is *Don't Stop*

Believin' by Journey. This timeless anthem reminds us of the resilience needed to keep pushing forward, no matter how many lives we've lived. Its lyrics, "Some will win, some will lose," echo the reality that in each phase of life, we encounter both success and failure, yet the journey continues. (Available on Spotify, Apple Music, and YouTube.)

Leaving a Legacy of Lives Lived

In the end, the legacy we leave behind is not the result of one life lived perfectly. It's the sum of all the lives we've lived—the transformations we've undergone, the lessons we've learned, and the people we've touched along the way. Our lives are a mosaic of experiences, and it's the variety, the reinventions, the beginnings and endings that create the rich tapestry of our existence.

The song *Changes* by David Bowie further encapsulates this theme. Bowie's timeless lyrics remind us that the only constant in life is change. With each reinvention, we grow closer to the person we are meant to be, and we leave behind a legacy not of stagnation, but of continual evolution. (Available on Spotify, Apple Music, and YouTube.)

By embracing the idea that we live many lives within one lifetime, we free ourselves from the fear of change. We give ourselves permission to evolve, to grow, and to chase new dreams without the guilt of abandoning the old ones. Life isn't about living one story—it's about living as many as you can, each one teaching you something new about who you are.

Takeaways

1. **Embrace Change**: Life is not linear, and change is a natural part of growth. Each new phase offers the opportunity to become someone new and more aligned with your true self.
2. **Let Go of Old Versions**: Holding onto past versions of yourself limits your potential. Let go of what no longer serves you to make room for new growth and transformation.
3. **Reinvention is a Gift**: Don't fear reinvention. It's a powerful tool that allows you to chase new dreams, explore new passions, and redefine success on your terms.
4. **Relationships Shape Us**: We live many lives through the people we love and connect with. Each deep relationship brings new experiences, perspectives, and growth into our lives.
5. **Trust the Journey**: Whether you win or lose, keep going. Life is about the journey, not the outcome. Keep evolving, and never stop believing in your ability to transform.

Media:

- *Film*: *The Curious Case of Benjamin Button* – Available on Netflix, Amazon Prime, and Disney+.
- *Music*: Fleetwood Mac – *Landslide* – Available on Spotify, Apple Music, and YouTube.
- *Music*: Journey – *Don't Stop Believin'* – Available on Spotify, Apple Music, and YouTube.
- *Music*: David Bowie – *Changes* – Available on Spotify, Apple Music, and YouTube.

Chapter 22

Self-Sufficiency – Road to Recovery

Self-sufficiency is not about standing alone against life's challenges but about cultivating the inner strength and resilience needed to weather the storms. It's about finding the capacity within us to rebuild, heal, and thrive even when the path forward seems arduous and uncertain.

The long road to recovery is a journey through uncharted territory, marked by obstacles, setbacks, and moments of despair. It's a road often traveled in solitude, where the scars of the past serve as a reminder of the trials endured. But it's also a road illuminated by the flicker of hope—a beacon that guides us toward healing and transformation.

So, what does self-sufficiency on the road to recovery entail?

The first step is acceptance—acknowledging the reality of your situation, including the pain and challenges it brings. Embrace your vulnerabilities and imperfections as part of your humanity.

Relatable Music

In moments of self-reflection, we often find ourselves waiting for clarity, much like *The Captain of Her Heart*. It speaks to the quiet patience required for self-discovery and recovery, reminding us that we must guide our own journey with gentle perseverance.

Artist	Title	Scan QR code
Double	The Captain of her heart	

Cultivate resilience as you face adversity. It's the ability to bounce back from setbacks and to adapt to new circumstances. Resilience is not a fixed trait but a skill that can be developed and strengthened over time.

Be kind to yourself throughout the journey. Self-compassion is the balm that soothes the wounds of the past. Treat yourself with the same care and empathy that you would offer to a dear friend.Recovery is a gradual process, often marked by small, incremental steps. Be

patient with yourself and recognize that healing takes time. Celebrate your progress, no matter how small it may seem. Set achievable, realistic goals that align with your recovery journey. These goals can provide direction and motivation as you move forward.

Celebrate your resilience and strength. Each day you wake up and continue the journey is a testament to your determination and courage.
The road to recovery is often a long and winding one, marked by moments of doubt and weariness. Yet, it is on this road that you uncover your inner fortitude, your capacity to heal, and your resilience in the face of life's most formidable challenges. As you walk this path of self-sufficiency and recovery, remember that it is not the destination that defines your journey but the profound transformation that occurs along the way.
The scars you bear are not symbols of weakness but badges of courage, testifying to your unwavering spirit and your indomitable will to rebuild, heal, and emerge stronger than before.

The journey may be long, but it is also a testament to the enduring human spirit—a journey that ultimately leads to a place of profound self-discovery, growth, and renewal. So, take each step with purpose and determination, for you are on the road to recovery - a journey that, in its challenges and triumphs, reveals the essence of your resilience and the beauty of your human spirit.

Relatable Music

Sometimes, the first step toward healing is allowing yourself to embrace love—whether from others or from within. *Step Inside Love* reminds us that recovery begins with the invitation to trust and open our hearts to new possibilities.

Artist	Title	Scan QR code
Cilla Black	**Step Inside Love**	

PART 8: MOMENTS OF CHANGE

These chapters examine the pivotal moments that compel us to reflect on our choices, take on transformation, and confront tasks that should not be delayed..

Chapter 23	**Ticking Clock** Explores the urgency of time and the necessity to act before opportunities slip away, encouraging readers to make the most of each moment
Chapter 24	**Tools for Transformation** Offers practical resources and insights for self-improvement, helping readers navigate transitions with resilience and purpose. *Embrace the Journey: Unleash Your Potential* *Practical Tools for Personal Growth* *Actionable Goal-Setting Templates* *Leading with Authenticity* *Navigating Career Transitions with Resilience* *Embracing Global Perspectives*
Chapter 25	**What You've Got to Lose?** Reflects on the importance of letting go of fear and taking risks, encouraging a mindset that values growth over comfort
Chapter 26	**What You Stand to Gain** Examines the benefits of embracing change and the personal growth that comes from stepping out of comfort zones *Personal Growth and Self-Discovery*

Chapter 23

Ticking Clock

In the grand orchestration of life, there's a relentless metronome that keeps its unwavering rhythm—the clock. It ticks away, second by second, minute by minute, an ever-present reminder of the finite nature of our existence. The sound can either haunt us or inspire us, depending on how we choose to perceive it.

It's that same relentless beat that echoes in *The Final Countdown* by Europe. As the clock ticks, the song's powerful, urgent energy propels us forward, reminding us that the countdown is always running—and now is the time to act, before time slips through our fingers.

Cue ***The Final Countdown*** by **Europe**.

Artist	**Title**	**Scan QR code**
Europe	**The final countdown**	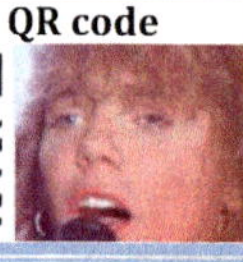

As the iconic anthem reverberates through our minds, it evokes a sense of urgency—a countdown toward something monumental, a moment where decisions cannot be postponed any longer. The clock ticks along, a constant companion on life's journey, urging us to make the most of the time we have left.

Yet, it's all too easy to become entangled in the busyness of life, to let the days slip by without truly living, without pursuing our dreams, or without spending time with those we hold dear. The countdown continues, and with every beat, we are reminded that time waits for no one.

So, what does the ticking of the clock mean for us, and how can we make the most of the time we have? The first step is awareness. Acknowledge that time is limited, and the moments we have are precious. Like the crescendo of Europe's anthem, use this awareness as motivation to live more intentionally and purposefully. Evaluate your priorities. What truly matters to you in life? What are your dreams, passions, and values? Align your actions with your priorities to make the most of your time.

Embrace opportunities as they come your way. Don't let fear or indecision hold you back. Seize the moment and take chances, for it's often through these experiences that we find the most profound growth and fulfilment. Invest in meaningful connections with loved ones. Time spent with family and friends is a treasure that enriches our lives immeasurably.

Even as *The Final Countdown* pushes us forward, it's a reminder that time shared with those who matter is never wasted.

The ticking of the clock need not be a source of anxiety; it can be a source of inspiration.

In the grand scheme, the sound of the ticking clock is our cue to play our part and appreciate the time we've been given. And as Europe's *The Final Countdown* echoes in the background, it's not just a reminder of time running out, but a call to action.

The stage is set, the spotlight is on us, and the music of life awaits our contribution. The question is, how will you choose to dance to its rhythm? **Relatable Music**

As the world moves forward, we are often reminded of the challenges that persist around us.

The World Is a Ghetto echoes the societal and personal struggles that accompany change, where we must navigate through both external and internal conflicts with resilience.

Artist	Title	Scan QR code
George Benson	**The World Is a Ghetto**	

Chapter 24

Tools for Transformation

Transformation is not only a journey of thought but also a journey of action. To cultivate resilience, authenticity, and personal growth, we must practice intentional steps every day. This chapter provides you with practical tools—worksheets, exercises, journaling prompts, and actionable templates—that will empower you to apply the principles from this book and make lasting changes in your life.

Embrace the Journey: Unleash Your Potential

As you step into this transformative path, it's important to recognize that growth isn't linear, but the energy driving it is boundless. Just like the spirit of Queen's iconic song, *Don't Stop Me Now*, your potential knows no limits.

Artist	Title	Scan QR code
Queen	Don't stop me now	

Embrace that unstoppable energy as you move forward.

Practical Tools for Personal Growth

Understanding transformation is only the first step; action is what solidifies change. Below, you'll find exercises designed to help you cultivate resilience, authenticity, and clarity as you grow.

Here are tips to enhance your resilience:

1. **Mindfulness Practices**: Engage in mindful breathing, meditation, or mindful movement each day to centre

yourself. These practices help you develop mental clarity and emotional balance, enabling you to navigate life's challenges with greater ease.

2. **Stress Management Techniques**: Incorporate techniques such as visualization, progressive muscle relaxation, and time management to handle stress effectively. These tools prevent burnout and empower you to stay resilient in high-pressure situations.

3. **Reframing Negative Thoughts**: Learn to identify and reframe unhelpful or negative thoughts. By changing the narrative, you tell yourself, you can transform setbacks into opportunities for growth.

Guided Journaling Prompts

Journaling offers a space for reflection and insight. The following prompts will help you document your journey:

- *What are the major challenges I've faced this week, and how have they helped me grow?*
- *What negative thoughts have surfaced, and how can I reframe them?*
- *What aspects of my life align with my core values, and where can I make changes to align further?*

Regular journaling deepens self-awareness and helps track your progress over time.

Actionable Goal-Setting Templates

Setting and achieving meaningful goals requires a clear plan. Use the SMART (Specific, Measurable, Achievable, Relevant, Time-bound) templates to break down your aspirations into manageable steps. These templates will help you turn your reflections into concrete actions, allowing you to continuously move forward.

Resilience and Authenticity in the Workplace

The principles of resilience and authenticity are not limited to personal growth—they are equally essential in professional life. Whether you're navigating career transitions or leading with integrity, resilience enables you to thrive in even the most high-pressure environments.

Maintaining Resilience in High-Pressure Environments

Work environments often test our resilience, especially in high-stakes industries. Here are strategies to help you build and maintain resilience at work:

- **Set Boundaries**: Define clear work-life boundaries to protect your mental and emotional health. Communicate these boundaries to your colleagues or superiors to manage expectations and prevent burnout.
- **Manage Stress Effectively**: Utilize stress-management techniques such as taking breaks, prioritizing tasks, and practicing mindfulness during the workday. These methods will enable you to perform at your best without compromising your well-being.
- **Cultivate Support Networks**: Build a network of supportive colleagues or mentors. Having a strong support system within the workplace provides a sense of security and shared resilience, especially during challenging times.

Leading with Authenticity

Authenticity in leadership is not just a personal trait—it's a professional advantage. Leaders who remain true to their values build trust, inspire teams, and create positive work environments. Here's how you can lead with authenticity:

- **Stay True to Your Values**: Authentic leaders are clear about their values and allow those principles to guide their decision-making.
- **Empower Others**: Foster a workplace where team members feel valued and supported. Encourage open dialogue, active listening, and empathy to create a more engaged and motivated workforce.
- **Adapt and Evolve**: Authentic leadership requires flexibility. As the workplace changes, so must your approach, but always in alignment with your core beliefs.

Navigating Career Transitions with Resilience

Career transitions- whether voluntary or unexpected—can feel daunting. By aligning your career with your core values and long-term goals, you ensure that these transitions lead to meaningful professional growth. Here's how:

- **Embrace Change**: View career shifts as opportunities for reinvention. Even challenging transitions can open doors to new paths that align more closely with your personal and professional aspirations.
- **Reflect on Values**: Periodically assess whether your current career reflects your values and long-term vision. Adjusting early will help you stay on track toward a fulfilling professional life.
- **Be Adaptable**: As career landscapes shift, so must your approach. Cultivate flexibility and openness to

new possibilities, allowing you to stay resilient and open to growth.

The Holistic Path to Resilience: Mind, Body, and Spirit
True resilience is holistic—it encompasses your mind, body, and spirit. Here's how you can nurture each area to maintain balance and navigate life's challenges.

Mindfulness and Mental Health
Mindfulness is a powerful tool for emotional resilience. Incorporate mindfulness practices such as meditation, mindful movement, and deep breathing into your daily routine. These practices create mental clarity, reduce stress, and enhance emotional well-being.

Physical Vitality and Emotional Resilience
Physical health is deeply tied to emotional well-being. Maintaining your physical vitality through exercise, balanced nutrition, and adequate sleep strengthens your emotional resilience. A healthy body supports a healthy mind, enabling you to face life's ups and downs with more energy and optimism.

Nurturing the Spirit
Spiritual well-being is just as important as mental and physical health. Engage in activities that bring joy and fulfilment, such as connecting with nature, practicing gratitude, or pursuing creative passions. These practices nourish the soul, helping you maintain a sense of purpose and balance, even during challenging times.

Embracing Global Perspectives: A Culturally Inclusive Approach to Growth
Personal growth is a universal pursuit, yet the ways in which we achieve it vary across cultures. By exploring

diverse perspectives, we can enrich our own understanding of resilience and authenticity.

Cultural Case Studies and Reflections

Resilience and authenticity are practiced differently around the world. By examining case studies from various cultures—where collectivist societies emphasize community support, or individualistic cultures stress self-reliance—we can see how universal themes of growth and well-being are interpreted through different lenses.

These stories remind us that while cultural contexts differ, the desire for a meaningful, balanced life is shared by all.

Takeaways

1. **Resilience is Holistic**: It's not limited to one aspect of life; resilience spans across personal growth, work, and overall well-being.
2. **Embrace Mindfulness**: Incorporating mindfulness into daily routines will strengthen your emotional resilience.
3. **Cultivate Authenticity**: Whether leading a team or navigating personal growth, authenticity is key to lasting fulfilment.
4. **Stay Adaptable**: Flexibility in both personal and professional settings is crucial for maintaining balance and navigating change.
5. **Nurture Your Spirit**: Taking care of your spiritual well-being is essential for long-term resilience and joy.

Chapter 25

What You've Got to Lose?

In every storm, there comes a moment when you stand at the edge, drenched in doubt, staring into the unknown. The wind howls, the waves crash, and you're faced with a choice: cling to the safety of the familiar or take a leap into the storm and risk it all. What have you really got to lose?

Throughout life, we find ourselves shackled by fear—fear of failure, fear of judgment, fear of loss. We hesitate, holding back from chasing our dreams or embracing change because the idea of losing what we know is terrifying. But what if we've been asking the wrong question all along? Instead of focusing on what we stand to lose, what if we asked: What do we stand to gain?

One of the most powerful representations of this struggle plays out in *Forrest Gump*. Lieutenant Dan, battling his inner demons, stands on the bow of a fishing boat, deep in the heart of a raging storm, screaming at the heavens, "Is that all you've got?" The storm reflects his fury—his sense of loss, hopelessness, and defiance. But something profound happens in that moment. As the winds rage and the waves crash, he lets go. He releases the anger, the fear, everything that has held him back. In doing so, he discovers a new kind of freedom.

That same emotional journey is captured in Samuel Barber's *Adagio for Strings.* The delicate notes build slowly, mirroring the tension we feel in moments of inner turmoil. As the music swells, it evokes the rising storm of emotions we face when we stand on the edge of everything familiar. The crescendo arrives, and with it, a profound resolution—

the realization that surrendering to the unknown can bring the greatest peace.
In the eye of the storm, everything feels like it's unravelling. The winds pull at your core, and the weight of all your fears and doubts presses in. You cling tightly to the familiar because letting go feels too risky. But as the storm rages on, something shifts—a moment of clarity breaks through, and you realize that in holding on, you're only feeding the storm. Like Lieutenant Dan, we all face storms.

We stand at crossroads, caught between fear and possibility. But it's not the storm that defines us - it's how we respond to it.

Adagio for Strings reminds us that letting go is not a sign of weakness; it's where we find our true strength. In surrendering, we make room for growth, for healing, for forward motion.

Artist	Title	Scan QR code
Samuel Barber	**Adagio for Strings**	

And yet, when fear of failure or judgment looms large, we often need a reminder to keep moving forward despite the noise.

Taylor Swift's *Shake It Off* is that anthem - a bold declaration to let go of the negativity that keeps us tethered. It's not about perfection; it's about resilience. The song's infectious energy shows us that sometimes, the best way to confront fear is simply to shake off the doubt and keep going. It's a light-hearted approach to a serious truth:

resilience is often the key to unlocking our greatest potential.

Fear of loss is a powerful force. It keeps us tethered to what's safe, what's known—but it also keeps us small. It convinces us that staying where we are is better than risking the unknown. But what if the greatest risk isn't in losing? What if it's in never trying?

Vangelis' *Chariots of Fire* embodies this exact spirit—the push beyond fear. The steady, rhythmic build of the music mirrors the heartbeat of every runner in the film, not striving merely to win, but to transcend.

The steady, rhythmic pulse of *Chariots of Fire* isn't just the beat of every runner - it's the heartbeat of everyone who dares to push beyond their limits.

Artist	Title	Scan QR code
Vangelis	***Chariots of fire***	

As the music builds, so does the sense of freedom that comes from letting go of fear. The crescendo isn't about victory over others; it's about victory over yourself.

Chariots of Fire reminds us that the real race is not against time or circumstance - it's against our own limitations. It's about breaking free of the boundaries we impose on ourselves. So, ask yourself:

What do you really have to lose?

The truth is, it's not about what you stand to lose—it's about what you stand to gain. The fear of loss can keep us tethered to the shore, but the real prize lies in stepping into the unknown, into the storm, and discovering the strength you never knew you had.

So, what will you choose? Will you let fear hold you back, or will you embrace the storm and all that lies beyond it? The question isn't what might you lose—it's what will you gain by risking it all?

Chapter 26

What You Stand to Gain

Personal Growth and Self-Discovery

Just as Lieutenant Dan found healing through his emotional storm, stepping out of your comfort zone allows you to confront your own inner conflicts. You gain the opportunity to grow, to stretch your limits, and to discover new aspects of yourself. It's in the challenges and uncertainties that you find the most profound opportunities for learning and transformation.

Relatable Music

As we journey through life, each step taken in resilience leads to incremental progress. Just like in Jeff Tysik's *Better and Better*, we move forward, one note at a time, improving steadily with every challenge we overcome.

Artist	Title	Scan QR code
Jeff Tysik	***Better and Better***	

Fulfilment and Purpose

Pursuing your dreams and passions leads to a sense of fulfilment and purpose that is incomparable. Life, at its core, is about the pursuit of what makes you come alive.

Resilience and Strength

Embracing change and taking risks cultivates resilience. Just like Lieutenant Dan on the boat, when you face life's storms head-on, you realize that you are stronger than you think. Each setback is a lesson, each challenge an opportunity to rise again. Resilience isn't just the ability to bounce back—it's the ability to adapt, grow, and emerge stronger than before.

New Connections and Relationships

Stepping into the unknown often leads to new connections and relationships. Just as the storm washed away Dan's bitterness, allowing him to finally open himself to new relationships and experiences, so too can your leap into the unknown open doors to people who share your values and dreams.

Wisdom and Perspective

Through the ups and downs of life, you gain wisdom and perspective. It's the knowledge that comes from lived experiences, from both successes and failures. Lieutenant Dan's storm is a powerful metaphor for the wisdom gained through adversity. Wisdom allows you to see that loss is not always negative—it's often a necessary part of growth.

Living Authentically

Taking chances allows you to live authentically. It's about being true to yourself and aligning your actions with your values and aspirations. You lose the facade of who you're supposed to be and gain the freedom to become who you are meant to be.

PART 9: DAYS OF RECKONING

In this section, we confront pivotal life reflections, focusing on unfulfilled potential and the evolving dynamics of love in a changing world.

Chapter 27 **Fear of Unfulfilled Potential**
Explores the emotional and mental toll of unmet aspirations, encouraging readers to overcome doubts and embrace their latent potential.
Letting go of fear
Building Resilience
Steps Toward Self-Fulfilment

Chapter 28 **Navigating Love in Our Changing World**
Examines the complexities of modern relationships, influenced by evolving cultural expectations, independence, and economic realities.
Marriage and Independence
Balancing Individuality and Connection
Embracing New Dynamics in Love

Chapter 27

Fear of Unfulfilled Potential

What you have to lose might not be tangible, but rather the realization that you never fully explored your potential. This is perhaps the greatest risk of all—the regret that accompanies a life lived in fear of taking risks. By staying in the safety of the familiar, you risk never discovering the full range of your capabilities.

In moments when the fear of **unfulfilled potential** weighs heavy, **Taylor Swift's *Shake It Off*** reminds you to let go of doubt, brush off negativity, and keep moving forward with confidence.

Artist	Title	Scan QR code
Shake It Off	Taylor Swift	

Consider this: the fear of loss is a natural human instinct, but it should not be the sole driving force in your life. Instead of dwelling on what might go wrong, focus on what might go right. Think about the experiences, growth, and fulfilment that await you on the other side of your fears. So, the next time you stand at a crossroads and wonder what you've got to lose, shift your perspective. Ask yourself what you've got to gain by taking that leap of faith, pursuing your dreams, or embracing change.

Learning from Spartacus

In life, as in the story of Spartacus, there are moments that call us to rise against seemingly insurmountable odds. Here was a man, a gladiator and slave, facing the might of an empire with nothing more than his iron will and a ragtag band of fellow fighters. If you think your Monday morning feels tough, imagine rallying an army with the sole mission to topple the world's superpower, armed with little more than sharpened determination and a few choice words.

Spartacus didn't have a five-year plan, but he had the fire to challenge Rome itself. In a way, he reminds us that the odds don't dictate our spirit; our spirit shapes the odds we choose to defy.

The real power of Spartacus wasn't just in his strength but in his relentless belief that freedom was worth every risk. Against all logic, every calculation, and every whispered doubt, he led others to dream beyond the chains they could see. Now, while our modern "battles" may be waged in boardrooms, cubicles, or during the daily grind, the lesson remains: sometimes, it's less about the size of the obstacle and more about the force of conviction behind our fight. After all, Spartacus teaches us that every insurmountable mountain is just a story waiting to be conquered—with the right mindset, a little humour, and the kind of spirit that refuses to stay silent.

The answers might surprise you, for it is often in the act of letting go of our fears that we discover the boundless potential of our lives. In the end, life's journey is not about holding onto what's safe; it's about letting go of what holds you back and stepping into the limitless possibilities of your own potential.

Musical Relevance Explained

Just as Lieutenant Dan's storm scene in ***Forrest Gump*** evokes themes of defiance, surrender, and ultimately inner peace, Samuel Barber's ***Adagio for Strings*** leads the listener through an emotional storm of their own. The music, slow and sorrowful at first, builds to a crescendo of emotional release, representing the internal struggle we all face when confronting our deepest fears. But just as the storm in ***Forrest Gump*** subsides, the tension in ***Adagio for Strings*** resolves into something quieter and more peaceful, symbolizing the catharsis that comes from letting go.

Find Your Strength

Together, these works remind us that confronting our fears and emotions head-on is not just a way to survive the storms of life - it's a path to discovering strength, clarity, and transformation. As we confront our fears of falling short, ***Sign of the Times*** captures the sombre reflection that accompanies those moments.

Artist	Title	Scan QR code
Bob James	Sign of the Times	

It reminds us that the ticking clock of life waits for no one, and the urgency to fulfil our potential grows with each passing moment. There comes a time in many of our journeys when we must face the truth that some things cannot be undone. *It's Too Late* captures the bittersweet realization that, despite our best efforts, we sometimes miss the moment.

Artist	Title	Scan QR code
Carole King	It's Too Late	

Chapter 28

Navigating Love in our Changing World

Marriage and Independence

In today's world, love and marriage have become more complex, with traditions challenged by evolving gender roles, cultural expectations, and economic realities. This chapter explores how independence, financial stability, and cultural values shape modern relationships, highlighting the new dynamics at play.

"Two of a Kind" **by Earl Klugh** captures the delicate balance of partnership and mutual understanding in relationships, much like the evolving dynamics of marriage today.

Artist	Title	Scan QR code
Earl Klugh	Two of a kind	

Empowerment Across Cultures

Women worldwide are more empowered than ever, though empowerment manifests differently across regions. In China and Japan, Confucian values still emphasize family over ambition, but urban women are redefining these roles. In the Middle East, marriage is often seen as a union between families, tied to social status, yet modern women, through education and careers, are slowly reshaping expectations.

In Northern Europe, societies like Sweden and Denmark lead the way in gender equality, supporting shared roles in both family and career. Southern Europe, influenced by the Catholic Church, is seeing delayed marriages and higher female workforce participation. In Eastern Europe and the Caribbean, tradition coexists with modern independence, balancing strong family ties with the rise of self-reliant women.

In the U.S., attitudes toward marriage vary widely. While conservative areas uphold traditional values, urban regions embrace individuality and delayed commitments, reflecting the country's cultural diversity.

The Evolving Dynamics of Marriage

Globally, marriage is no longer the inevitable cornerstone of life. In Japan and China, declining marriage and birth rates reflect the pressures of modern life. The Middle East sees a similar tension, as women push for personal fulfilment while navigating deeply ingrained traditions. Northern Europe's progressive policies provide a model for balancing independence and family without losing stability.

Southern and Eastern Europe, like the Caribbean, show a growing acceptance of cohabitation and delayed marriage.

These regions reflect a broader trend of valuing personal fulfilment alongside family commitment, while in the U.S., marriage is increasingly shaped by the interplay of tradition and progressive ideals.

Marriage as a Contract: Love 'Ltd or Inc'

What if we reframed marriage as a corporate merger? Imagine a marriage contract written like a business agreement: "Party A agrees to a 50% stake in household chores, with performance bonuses tied to relationship milestones such as anniversaries, birthdays, and successfully navigating the in-laws at Christmas. Failure to meet the agreed-upon KPIs (Key Partner Indicators) will result in renegotiation or amicable dissolution—complete with severance pay."

This playful metaphor underscores the increasing use of prenuptial agreements and the pragmatic approach to marriage today. Just like in business, planning for the worst while hoping for the best is not pessimism—it's prudence. Love, like any partnership, thrives on clear expectations and careful planning, ensuring both parties can weather life's challenges together.

Relatable Music

The Lady In My Life encapsulates the importance of emotional vulnerability and creating a sanctuary of love, even amidst the chaos of modern relationships. Love, at its core, often brings with it questions of uncertainty and timing.

Artist	Title	Scan QR code
Michael Jackson	The Lady In My Life	

When Will I See You Again? speaks to the longing and vulnerability that often accompany modern relationships, reflecting the emotional crossroads we face when navigating love in unpredictable times.

Artist	Title	Scan QR code
The Three Degrees	When Will I See You Again	

Digital Love: Swipe Right to Mrs. Right

In the age of dating apps, the search for a soulmate is as easy as a swipe. But with great convenience comes great indecision—if you can scroll through a catalogue of potential partners, how do you know when to stop?

The paradox of choice means that finding "**the one**" has never been more accessible, yet more elusive. As some might joke, "Why settle down when the next swipe could be a CEO with a six-pack and a love for puppies?"

This modern-day dilemma underscores a broader truth: technology has transformed not just how we meet but how we choose.

The digital age offers more options than ever before, but it also brings new challenges in decision-making and commitment. The humour lies in treating love like online shopping, but the underlying issue is the real struggle to find satisfaction and certainty in a world of endless possibilities.

And while the swipes continue, **Candi Staton's *Young Hearts Run Free*** strikes a chord for those caught in the whirlwind of modern romance.

It's easy to get swept up in the search for "the one" when options seem infinite, but Staton's anthem reminds us that love should never come at the cost of personal freedom or self-worth.

Artist	Title	Scan QR code
Candi Staton	***Young Hearts Run Free***	

Sometimes, the best swipe you can make is swiping right on yourself—choosing independence over settling for less. In the era of dating apps, it's a message that's more relevant than ever.

Fatherhood and Financial Responsibility

The impact of marriage breakdowns varies across cultures. In Asia and the Middle East, divorce rates remain low, but when divorce happens, the financial burden, often on men, is significant. Northern Europe promotes shared financial and custodial responsibility, while Southern Europe and the Caribbean rely on extended families for support.

In the U.S., varying divorce laws and costly settlements often deter men from marrying, reflecting concerns about the financial risks associated with long-term commitments.

Attraction and Selection: A Global View

Attraction and mate selection, though rooted in biology, are heavily influenced by culture. In Asia, modesty and family expectations guide relationships, but modern shifts emphasize personal compatibility. The Middle East still upholds traditional values like modesty and honour, but younger generations seek emotional connection.

Northern Europe champions autonomy and equality, while Southern and Eastern Europe balance tradition and modern values.

The Caribbean, with its blend of tradition and independence, reflects flexible approaches to relationships. In the U.S., attraction is shaped by diverse cultural norms, ranging from traditional to individualistic ideals.

Let Your Love Flow: An Anthem for Love

Artist	Title	Scan QR code
The Bellamy Brothers	***Let Your Love Flow***	

Through all the complexities of modern relationships whether in marriage, digital dating, or balancing independence - there remains a simple truth: love is at its best when it flows freely.

The Bellamy Brothers' song *Let Your Love Flow* captures this sentiment perfectly.

Its upbeat, joyful message reminds us that despite the changing dynamics of love, the key is to keep it natural, unburdened, and genuine. The song serves as a reminder to allow love to flourish, even amid modern-day challenges like navigating technology, cultural expectations, or personal ambition.

Takeaways

1. **Empowerment and Autonomy**: Independence is a cornerstone of modern relationships, though it plays out differently across cultures.

2. **Cultural and Financial Factors**: Economic realities and cultural shifts shape marriage dynamics globally, with financial considerations playing a major role.

3. **Evolving Gender Roles**: Changing roles call for new approaches to equality and partnership, though the pace of change varies.

4. **Communication**: Clear, respectful communication is vital for relationship success across cultures.

5. **Legal Protections**: The rise of prenuptial agreements reflects a pragmatic approach to safeguarding modern relationships.

Relatable Films:

Marriage Story (2019)

Noah Baumbach's *Marriage Story* captures the raw complexity of modern relationships, exploring autonomy, career ambition, and the emotional toll of separation, perfectly aligning with the themes discussed in this chapter.

- *Kramer vs. Kramer* (1979): Explores the emotional and financial toll of divorce.

- *A Streetcar Named Desire* (1951): A cautionary tale on power dynamics in relationships.

- *Scenes from a Marriage* (1973): Delves into the complexity of long-term relationships.

- *The Way We Were* (1973): Examines love and personal ambition.

- *An Unmarried Woman* (1978): Focuses on female independence and self-discovery.

- *Who's Afraid of Virginia Woolf?* (1966): A powerful look at emotional complexity in marriage.

FINAL THOUGHTS

In the end, life offers no shortcuts—not in love, not in marriage, and not in finding your way through the complex paths we walk.

Whether navigating global traditions, drawing up contracts, or simply swiping through the digital ocean in search of connection, one truth remains: the heart takes its time. And perhaps that's the point.

The twists and turns, the missteps, the unexpected detours—they aren't obstacles. They are the journey. Every challenge, moment of doubt, and hard-earned victory shapes us into who we're meant to become. The greatest reward lies not in reaching the end but in walking the path, hand in hand, with those who matter.

Yazz's *"The Only Way Is Up"* reminds us that no matter how low we go, we rise.

Artist	Title	Scan QR code
Yazz	***The only way is up***	

We rise from love, hope, and the belief that tomorrow holds more than today. When life pulls us down, this anthem becomes a reminder: we are never defeated, only delayed.

Les McCann's timeless song ***"With These Hands"*** captures this same truth.

Artist	Title	Scan QR code
Les Macan	*With these hands*	

What we build—our relationships, our growth, our legacy—is crafted not through shortcuts, but with care, resilience, and heart. Life's most precious rewards don't come easy; they come when we show up, day after day, giving everything we've got.
And just like Eurythmics' ***"Sweet Dreams"***, the pursuit of dreams is not without its challenges.

Artist	Title	Scan QR code
Eurythmics	Sweet Dreams	

The road may be unclear, with some trying to use us and others holding us back - but through it all, we press forward. Sweet dreams are made of persistence, resilience, and the courage to walk through life on your own terms. In the end, success isn't about winning the race. It's about rising every time we fall, loving even when it's hard, and embracing the journey fully. Life's greatest magic isn't in where we end up, but in how we live and who we become along the way.

Yes, there are shortcuts - just *avoid* them. Take the *long* road. Love fiercely. Rise each time you fall, because **the *only way is up.***
And never forget what ***sweet dreams are made of***!

APPENDIX A: SONG LIST

To fully immerse yourself in *No Short Cuts*, you can listen to music and watch selected film clips that align with each section of the book. Simply scan the QR code or visit www.noshortcuts.co.uk/noshortcuts-media. The playlist follows the exact order of the references in the book, allowing you to experience each piece naturally as you read.

For easy use, keep your phone alongside the book, so you can play each piece by clicking on the artist or scene image without needing to switch back and forth. This synchronized multimedia playlist brings the narrative to life, blending sound and visuals with every chapter.

1. **Dave Brubeck - Take 5**
   Preface, Page: 7
   Narrative: Offbeat and unexpected, yet undeniably smooth -reflecting the rhythm of life itself.

2. **Tear for Fears, - Everybody was a bit in the middle of the book where I'm just a bitwants to rule the world**
   Preface, Page 8
   Narrative: captures the internal struggle between ambition and acceptance, control and surrender.

3. **The Alan Parsons Project - Eye in the sky**
   Preface, Page 9
   Narrative: embodies themes of silent authority and calm detachment symbolizing a higher, unseen force ,fate, destiny, or a watchful presence

4. **Al Pacino - Scent of a Woman (1992)**
   Preface, Page: 9
   Narrative: Lieutenant Colonel Frank Slade's speech emphasizes the irreparable damage to one's spirit from choices we regret or principles we've abandoned.

5. **Russell Crowe - Gladiator (2000)**
   Preface, Page: 10
   Narrative: the music rises and falls like the tides of resilience – finding the strength to rise again.

6. **Johan Sebastian Bach-cello number one in G Major**
   Preface, Page: 10
   Narrative: Mirrors life's journey, demanding evolution through obstacles, not anticipated. 12.

7. **Arvo Pärt - Spiegel im Spiegel**
   Preface, Page: 11
   Narrative: A minimalist masterpiece reflecting the journey from turmoil to calm.

8. **Pat Metheny - The truth will always be**
   Preface, Page: 12
   Narrative: Tranquility in spaces between certainty and doubt.

9. **Ludwig van Beethoven - Symphony 9, Ode to Joy**
   Abstract, Page: 14
   Narrative: True joy earned through perseverance

10. **Bill Withers - Lovely Day**
    Abstract, Page: 15
    Narrative: A feel-good song to celebrate small moments of joy and perseverance.

11. **Claude Debussy - Clair De Lune**
    Meet the Author, Page: 16
    Narrative: Subtle and profound doors of empathy

12. **Miles Davis - Kind of Blue**
    Meet the Author, Page: 16
    Narrative: The improvisational nature mirrors life's unpredictability and the beauty of adaptability.

13. **Anne Sophie Mutter -Sebelius in D minor up.47 Allegro moderato**
    Meet the Author, Page: 17
    Narrative: The emotional depth and complexity of life

14. **Elton John - Philadelphia freedom**
    Meet the Author, Page: 17
    Narrative: Balance between structure and spontaneity

15. **Gloria Gaynor - I Will Survive**
    Meet the Author, Page: 18
    Narrative: This track reflects overcoming emotional hardship and personal growth.

16. **Pat Metheny - Always and Forever**
    Meet the Author, Page: 18
    Narrative: A poignant, expansive melody symbolizing life's balance between intimate and vast experiences.

17. **Led Zeppelin - Stairway to Heaven**
    Meet the Author, Page: 19
    Narrative: Reflects the winding journey of life, the choices we make, and the search for meaning beyond material gain.

18. **Ludwig van Beethoven - Symphony No.5**
A journey like no other, Page: 21
Narrative: capturing the feeling of life's unexpected knocks symbolising fate itself.

19. **Gustav Holst - Jupiter, the Bringer of Jollity**
A journey like no other, Page: 22
Narrative: Holst's triumphant melody reflects the joy and growth that comes from fully embracing uncertainties.

20. **Ludovico Einaudi - Experience**
A journey like no other, Page: 25
Narrative: compliments the tattooist concept of going with the flow and finding balance.

21. **Carly Simon - "Nobody Does It Better"**
Grand Odyssey, Page: 26
Narrative: A track celebrating personal excellence and self-worth.

22. **Roxy Music - Don't stop the dance**
Grand Odyssey, Page: 27
Narrative: no matter what the obstacles keep moving not 20 or absolutely correct so where do I start?

23. **The Mamas & the Papas - California Dreamin**
Chapter 1, Page: 30
Narrative: Reflects the deep yearning for change and a brighter future.

24. **a-ha - Take On Me**
Chapter 1, Page: 31
Narrative: A high-energy anthem of optimism and seizing opportunities.

25. **Erik Satie - Gymnopédie No. 1**
Chapter 1, Page: 33
Narrative: Satie's reflective piece highlights moments of introspection.

26. **Freddie Hubbard - Little Sunflower**
Chapter 1, Page: 33
Narrative: This jazz composition reflects the need to remain adaptable and trust the journey.

27. **Shirley Bassey-Where do I begin?**
Chapter 1, Page: 34
Narrative: haunting song mirroring the uncertainty, we all face beginning something new.

28. **Stavros Lantsias – Diary of dreams**
Chapter 1, Page: 34
Narrative: Delicate Melody highlighting quiet moments of vulnerability

29. **Pat Metheny – Passaggio per il Paradiso**
Chapter 1, Page: 35
Narrative: uplifting Melody with message of hope

30. **Michael Jackson – Man in the mirror**
Chapter 2, Page: 36
Narrative: Being objective about our flaws and virtues

31. **The Beatles - Let It Be**
Chapter 2, Page: 38
Narrative: The song echoes themes of letting go and embracing peace amidst adversity.

32. **Spandau Ballet - True**
Chapter 2, Page: 41

Narrative: Celebrating personal excellence and self-worth.

33. **Lady Gaga - Born This Way**
Chapter 2, Page: 42
Narrative: An anthem about embracing individuality and living authentically.

34. **Coldplay - Talk**
Chapter 2, Page: 46
Narrative: Reflecting the importance of open communication in navigating relationships.

35. **Pink Floyd - Another Brick in the Wall**
Chapter 3, Page: 55
Narrative: A powerful anthem of resistance and individuality, challenging authority and conformity, symbolizing the journey toward personal freedom and self-discovery.

36. **Terry Jacks - Seasons in the Sun**
Chapter 3, Page: 56
Narrative: A nostalgic and bittersweet song capturing reflections on life, love, and farewell, echoing the transient beauty of seasons and moments.

37. **Joni Mitchel – Both sides now**
Chapter 3, Page: 60
Narrative: Bittersweet realisation of life's most cherished illusions

38. **Nina Simone - Feeling good**
Chapter 3, Page: 70
Narrative: Feeling of renewal and emotional freedom from rejuvenation

39. **George Michael - You've changed**
Chapter 3, Page: 72
Narrative: Bittersweet transformation changed by emotions.

40. **Bill Kong, Hsu Li Kong, Ang Lee - Crouching tiger hidden Dragon**
Chapter 3, Page: 73
Narrative: Emotional weight of hidden responsibilities and desires

41. **George Michael - Careless Whisper**
Chapter 3, Page: 75
Narrative: This song mirrors Emma's internal conflict, knowing she had to move forward but still mourning the past.

42. **Fleetwood Mac - Landslide**
Chapter 3, Page: 76
Narrative: Reflects the passage of time and personal transformation.

43. **Daft Punk - Digital Love**
Chapter 3, Page: 79
Narrative: A song reflecting the balance between connection and disconnection in modern love.

44. **Mick Hucknall - Holding Back the Years**
Chapter 3, Page: 81
Narrative: Echoes the unspoken grief of watching the passage of time.

45. **Eva Cassidy - Fields of Gold**
Chapter 3, Page: 82

Narrative: A reminder of golden moments shared in life's journey.

46. **Kylie Minogue - Spinning Around**
Chapter 3, Page: 90
Narrative: Mirrors personal reinvention and rediscovery.

47. **Richard Strauss - Sprach Zarathustra**
Chapter 3, Page: 93
Narrative: A powerful orchestral piece mirroring the philosophical journey of seeking purpose and meaning

48. **Ramsay Lewis - The Sun Goddess**
Chapter 4, Page: 104
Narrative: Reflective and soothing, this track guides the reader through emotional healing and growth

49. **Sinead O'Connor -Thank you for hearing me**
Chapter 4, Page: 106
Narrative: About being heard, seen and truly understood

50. **Pink Martini - Sing**
Chapter 4, Page: 107
Narrative: A joyous celebration of life and the courage to embrace your voice.

51. **David Sanbourn Rain on Christmas**
Chapter 4, Page: 109
Narrative: Evokes a sense of warmth and introspection

52. **Sweet - Blockbuster**
Chapter 6, Page: 119

Narrative: High-energy and fun, this track reflects the boldness of stepping into the spotlight.

53. **Level 42 - Something about you**
    Chapter 6, Page: 125
    Narrative: reflects uncertainty that accompanies conflict in close relationships

54. **Bob James - Angela (Theme from Taxi)**
    Chapter 6, Page: 128
    Narrative: Reflective piece symbolizing quiet strength found in everyday life.

55. **Shirley Bassey - I Am What I Am**
    Chapter 7, Page: 130
    Narrative: Empowering anthem celebrating self-acceptance and authenticity.

56. **Simon and Garfunkel - The Sound of silence**
    Chapter 7, Page: 133, Chapter 18, Page: 216
    Narrative: The power of quiet moments when no one knows what you are thinking.

57. **Marvin Gaye & Tammi Terrell - Ain't No Mountain High Enough**
    Chapter 7, Page: 133
    Narrative: A song of determination, persistence, and inner strength.

58. **ABBA - The winner takes it all**
    Chapter 7, Page: 134
    Narrative: How winning throws a light on the stagnation of others

59. **Queen - We are the champions**
Chapter 7, Page: 134
Narrative: Declaration of victory from relentless focus and hard work

60. **Christopher Cross - Sailing**
Chapter 8, Page: 138
Narrative: Navigating emotional turbulence with peace and clarity.

61. **Seal - Crazy**
Chapter 8, Page: 139
Narrative: Laments the notion that we need to be somewhat detached from reality

62. **R.E.M – Everybody Hurts**
Chapter 8, Page: 140
Narrative: reflects moments of isolation and pain for everyone universally.

63. **Chaka Khan-I'm every woman**
Chapter 8, Page: 146
Narrative: declaration of a woman's multifaceted power.

64. **Gloria Gaynor-I will survive**
Chapter 8, Page: 148
Narrative: anthem of resilience.

65. **Duran Duran - Reflex**
Chapter 9, Page: 152
Narrative: Instantaneous and involuntary response to an environment all group of people.

66. **Deodato - Night Cruiser**
Chapter 9, Page: 154
Narrative: A smooth ride through life's mysteries, combining rhythm and introspection.

67. **David Bowie - Space Oddity**
Chapter 9, Page: 154
Narrative: Captures the feeling of isolation that technology can foster.

68. **Vangelis - Blade Runner Blues**
Chapter 9, Page: 155
Narrative: A haunting, atmospheric reflection on solitude and the urban landscape.

69. **Jamiroquai - Virtual Insanity**
Chapter 10, Page: 156
Narrative: Captures the irony of a world that offers freedom through technology but also leaves us disconnected from authentic experiences.

70. **Fleetwood Mac - Go your own way**
Chapter 10, Page: 158
Narrative: Captures the spirit of independence.

71. **T Rex - Get it on**
Chapter 10, Page: 158
Narrative: captures the notion of freedom and the emotional cost of this lifestyle

72. **Dusty Springfield - Son of a preacher man**
Chapter 11, Page: 160
Narrative: Spiritual doctrines versus or morality

73. **Gregory Porter - It could've been me**
Chapter 11, Page: 161
Narrative: Reflects on the role fate plays in our lives

74. **Amy Winehouse - Rehab**
Chapter 12, Page: 166
Narrative: story of defiance and resistance to rehabilitation

75. **Adele - Skyfall**
Chapter 12, Page: 170
Narrative: protagonist rising from overwhelming odds

76. **Survivor - Eye of the tiger**
Chapter 12, Page: 171
Narrative: Facing challenges head on with a surge of energy

77. **Hot Chocolate - You Sexy Thing**
Chapter 12, Page: 171
Narrative: A fun, energetic addition that celebrates confidence and self-love.

78. **Fantastic woman - Queen**
Chapter 13, Page: 180
Narrative: haunting and beautiful in the struggles faced by LGBTQ individuals in a world that is often unkind to difference.

79. **Kool and the Gang - Summer Madness**
Chapter 13, Page: 180
Narrative: A smooth, reflective instrumental capturing the hazy warmth of summer.

80. **Donna Summer - Love to Love You Baby**
Chapter 13, Page: 181
Narrative: A sensual anthem exploring the passionate, intimate side of love.

81. **George Benson - Give Me the Night**
Chapter 13, Page: 184
Narrative: Captures the allure and excitement of nightlife, celebrating freedom and joy.

82. **Soft Cell - Tainted Love**
Chapter 13, Page: 184
Narrative: Reflects the darker side of love and relationships, marked by emotional conflict.

83. **Ralph Vaughan Williams - The Lark Ascending**
Chapter 14, Page: 188
Narrative: A soothing reflection on embracing uncertainty and emotional clarity.

84. **Blue Öyster Cult - Don't fear the reaper**
Chapter 15, Page: 192
Narrative: letting go of fear to challenge the unknown as a necessary step towards progress.

85. **The Lost Boys - Cry Little Sister**
Chapter 16, Page: 201
Narrative: haunting and soulful melody captures deep internal struggle between darkness and self realisation.

86. **Youn Sun Nah - Voyage**
Chapter 17, Page: 207
Narrative: Evokes introspection and infinite wonder, reflecting life's emotional journey.

87. **Rimsky-Korsakov - Scheherazade: The Young Prince**
Chapter 17, Page: 207
Narrative: A richly woven tale of love and adventure, embodying passion and intrigue.

88. **Gheorghe Zamfir & James Last - "The Lonely Shepherd"**
Chapter 18, Page: 210
Narrative: A haunting melody that reflects solitude and introspection.

89. **The Jones Girls - Children of the Night**
Chapter 18, Page: 216
Narrative: Reflects the power and mystery of night, embracing resilience in the face of adversity.

90. **Ella Fitzgerald - Summertime**
Chapter 19, Page: 218
Narrative: A timeless melody that reflects the easy, relaxed nature of life's slower moments

91. **Loose Ends - Slow Down**
Chapter 19, Page: 220
Narrative: Savouring the moment to step back and appreciate what's here now

92. **Mozart - Le nozze di Figaro, K.492, Act 3: Sull'aria**
Chapter 20, Page: 225
Narrative: A light duet representing delicate balance and cooperation in relationships.

93. **Matt Munro - On Days Like These**
Chapter 20, Page: 228

Narrative: Evokes the bittersweet beauty of fleeting moments, highlighting the passage of time.

94. **Massive Attack - Unfinished symphony**
Chapter 21, Page: 229
Narrative: captures the sense of evolution occurring due to the unfinished nature of a journey.

95. **Pharrell Williams - Happy**
Chapter 21, Page: 230
Narrative: captures the the art of reinvention whilst embracing happiness and joy

96. **Double - The Captain of Her Heart**
Chapter 22, Page: 237
Narrative: A smooth, melodic reflection on love, loss, and quiet resilience.

97. **Cilla Black - Step Inside Love**
Chapter 22, Page: 239
Narrative: Inviting warmth, this song reflects the joy of welcoming love and connection.

98. **Europe - The final countdown**
Chapter 23, Page: 241
Narrative: The time to act before time slips through our fingers - iconic anthem.

99. **George Benson - The World Is a Ghetto**
Chapter 23, Page: 243
Narrative: A deep, soulful track reflecting the complexity of life in a challenging world.

100. **Queen – Don't Stop Me Now**
Chapter 24, Page: 244

Narrative: embracing the unstoppable energy to move forward.

101. **Samuel Barber - Adagio for Strings**
Chapter 25, Page: 251
Narrative: where letting go is not a sign of weakness

102. **Vangelis – Chariots of fire**
Chapter 25, Page: 252
Narrative: sense of freedom that comes from letting go of fear. Pushing the limits.

103. **Jeff Tysik - Better and Better**
Chapter 26, Page: 254
Narrative: A celebration of progress, reflecting growth and self-improvement.

104. **Taylor Swift - Shake it off**
Chapter 27, Page: 257
Narrative: letting go of doubt shaking off negativity

105. **Bob James - Sign of the times**
Chapter 27, Page: 259
Narrative: sombre reflection of fear of falling short

106. **Carole King - It's Too Late**
Chapter 27, Page: 259
Narrative: Reflects the ending of a relationship, highlighting acceptance and moving forward.

107. **Earl Klugh - Two of a kind**
Chapter 28, Page: 260
Narrative: captures the delicate balance of a partnership and mutual understanding

108. **Michael Jackson - The Lady In My Life**
Chapter 28, Page: 262
Narrative: A soft, intimate tribute to love and tenderness, bringing emotional depth to personal connections.

109. **The Three Degrees - When will I see you again?**
Chapter 28, Page: 263
Narrative: emotional vulnerability that often accompanies modern relationships.

110. **Candy Staton - Young hearts run free**
Chapter 28, Page: 264
Narrative: emotional vulnerability that often accompanies modern relationships.

111. **The Bellamy Brothers - Let your love flow**
Chapter 28, Page: 265
Narrative: Anthem for love to flourish

112. **Yazz – The only way is up!**
Final Thoughts, Page: 268
Narrative: Launch-pad for the brighter future.

113. **Les Macan – With these hands**
Final Thoughts, Page: 269
Narrative: heartfelt growth and legacy.

114. **The Eurythmics – Sweat Dreams**
Final Thoughts, Page: 269
Narrative: what dreams can be made of

APPENDIX B: MOVIES

1. **Scent of a Woman (1992)**
   Chapter: *Preface*
   Page: 9
   Narrative: Lieutenant Colonel Frank Slade's speech emphasizes the irreparable damage to one's spirit from choices we regret or principles we've abandoned.

2. **The Shawshank Redemption (1994)**
   Chapter: *Life Lessons Through the Camera*
   Page: 51
   Narrative: Andy Dufresne's unyielding hope exemplifies resilience in the face of adversity, aligning with the book's themes of perseverance and integrity.

3. **Dead Poets Society (1989)**
   Chapter: *Life Lessons Through the Camera*
   Page: 51
   Narrative: The film's "Carpe Diem" message urges us to seize the day and live a life true to our values, similar to the themes of self-awareness and authenticity explored in the book.

4. **A Beautiful Mind (2001)**
   Chapter: *Life Lessons Through the Camera*
   Page: 51
   Narrative: John Nash's triumph over schizophrenia highlights the power of love and support, emphasizing the book's focus on resilience and relationships.

5. **Forrest Gump (1994)**
   Chapter: *Life Lessons Through the Camera*

Page: 52
Narrative: Forrest Gump's simple, honest approach to life is a testament to the power of authenticity and staying true to oneself despite life's complexities.

6. **The Matrix (1999)**
   Chapter: *Life Lessons Through the Camera*
   Page: 52
   Narrative: Neo's choice between illusion and harsh reality mirrors the journey of awakening to one's true self and the courage required to face the truth.

7. **The Godfather (1972)**
   Chapter: *Life Lessons Through the Camera*
   Page: 53
   Narrative: Michael Corleone's transformation explores loyalty, power, and the challenges of staying true to one's values.

8. **It's a Wonderful Life (1946)**
   Chapter: *Life Lessons Through the Camera*
   Page: 53
   Narrative: George Bailey's realization of his worth reflects the book's themes of self-worth and living a life aligned with one's values.

9. **Good Will Hunting (1997)**
   Chapter: *Life Lessons Through the Camera*
   Page: 52
   Narrative: Will's journey to trust himself, despite past traumas, aligns with the book's message of self-compassion and vulnerability.

10. **The Devil Wears Prada (2006)**
    Chapter 3: *Career Crossroads*

Page: 59
Narrative: Sarah's career conflict mirrors the existential questions faced by the film's protagonist, questioning whether success is worth personal sacrifice.

11. **The Secret Life of Walter Mitty (2013)**
    Chapter 3: *Scenario 2 - Career Transition*
    Page: 61
    Narrative: Walter's leap into adventure and self-discovery mirrors the book's message of following personal aspirations over societal expectations.

12. **The Lost Boys (1987)**
    Chapter 16 : *Do you Trust yourself*
    Page: 201
    Narrative: The song "Cry Little Sister" from the film captures the struggle between fear and self-realization, reflecting the emotional tension of self-trust.

13. **A Fantastic Woman (2017)**
    Chapter: *LGBTQ+ Resilience*
    Page: 180
    Narrative: Marina's journey of facing societal rejection reflects the themes of resilience and identity explored in the book.

14. **The Danish Girl (2015)**
    Chapter: *The Courage to Transform*
    Page: 181
    Narrative: Lili Elbe's transition explores identity, love, and courage, aligning with the themes of personal transformation in the book.

15. **The Mission (1986)**
    Chapter 11: *Does Religion or Faith Matter*
    Page: 163
    Narrative: The film's exploration of faith and moral conviction mirrors the internal battles faced by individuals searching for meaning amidst adversity.

16. **The Truman Show (1998)**
    Chapter 15: Are you afraid of your life?
    Page: 193
    Narrative: Truman's escape from his false reality mirrors the theme of confronting fear to live an authentic life.

17. **Parenthood (1989)**
    Chapter 3 – Scenario 7: *Empty Nest*
    Page: 86
    Narrative: The film explores the emotional transition as children grow up and leave home, reflecting the themes of identity and rediscovery explored in the book.

APPENDIX C: CULTURAL INFO

1. **Rumi – Persian Poet**
   Quote: *"It's your road and yours alone. Others may walk it with you, but no one can walk it for you."*
   Significance: This quote emphasizes the deeply personal nature of each individual's life journey, highlighting the importance of self-reliance and personal growth.
   Chapter: *Introduction (A Journey Like No Other)*
   Platforms: Available in Rumi's poetry collections, online literary sources, and various books on Persian poetry.

2. **Buddhist Teaching – Impermanence (Anicca)**
   Concept: *Anicca (Impermanence)* – The idea that everything is in constant flux and change is the only constant in life.
   Significance: Embracing the concept of impermanence helps us grow through life's inevitable changes, especially in personal relationships and identity struggles.
   Chapter: *Emma's Story (The Complexity of Growth and Tradition)*
   Platforms: Available in texts like *The Dhammapada* and Buddhist teachings on mindfulness and resilience.

3. **African Proverb – Perseverance**
   Proverb: *"Smooth seas do not make skilful sailors."*
   Significance: This African proverb speaks to the importance of facing challenges to develop resilience and grow in life. It's a reminder that hardships shape our skills and character.

Chapter: *Jake and Mia's Story (Navigating Love in the Digital Age)*

4. **Taoist Philosophy – Wu Wei (Effortless Action)**
   Concept: *Wu Wei* – A Taoist principle that encourages finding balance by going with the natural flow of life rather than resisting it.
   Significance: This philosophy teaches that growth and personal success are more easily achieved when we align ourselves with life's natural rhythms, allowing things to unfold naturally.
   Chapter: *Conclusion (Life is the Journey)*

5. **Eastern Philosophy – Non-Attachment**
   Concept: *Non-Attachment* – A principle from Hindu and Buddhist teachings that suggests freedom comes from releasing expectations and desires.
   Significance: Letting go of attachments allows personal freedom and growth, especially when it comes to relationships and personal desires.
   Chapter: *Emma's Story (The Complexity of Growth and Tradition)*
   Platforms: Available in Hindu and Buddhist philosophy books, such as *The Bhagavad Gita* and *The Dhammapada*.

6. **Sufi Wisdom – Patience and Perseverance**
   Quote: *"Patience is not sitting and waiting, it is foreseeing. It is looking at the thorn and seeing the rose, looking at the night and seeing the day."*
   Significance: Sufi wisdom teaches us that true patience is visionary—it's about enduring challenges while keeping sight of future potential and the beauty that follows hardship.

Chapter: *Reflective Chapter on Career and Personal Growth*
Platforms: Available in Sufi literature, such as the works of Rumi, Hafiz, and modern Sufi teachings.

Additional Platforms for Cultural and Philosophical Exploration:

- **Books:**
    - *The Tao Te Ching* (Taoist Philosophy)
    - *The Dhammapada* (Buddhist Teachings)
    - *The Bhagavad Gita* (Hindu Philosophy)
    - *Rumi: The Book of Love* (Persian Poetry)
    - *African Wisdom* (Collections of African Proverbs)
    - *The Essential Rumi* (Sufi Teachings)
- **Online Resources:**
    - Access to free philosophical texts and teachings via websites like *Sacred-Texts.com*, *Project Gutenberg*, and *Open Library*.
    - Audio lectures on Eastern and Western philosophy on platforms such as *Audible*, *Spotify*, and *YouTube*.

APPENDIX D: CURATED PLAYLIST

No Short Cuts Website Link